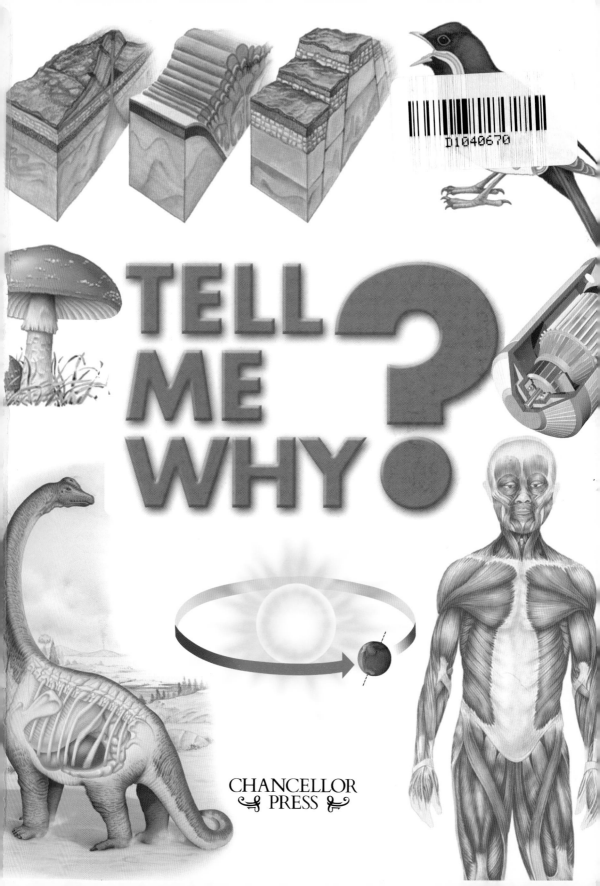

TELL ME WHY?

CHANCELLOR
PRESS

This edition first published
in 2002 by Bounty Books,
a division of Octopus Publishing Group Ltd.,
Endeavour House, 189 Shaftesbury Avenue,
London WC2H 8JY
www.octopusbooks.co.uk

An Hachette UK Company
www.hachette.co.uk

ISBN: 978-0-753704-43-1

Printed in China

CONTENTS

THE

HUMAN BODY

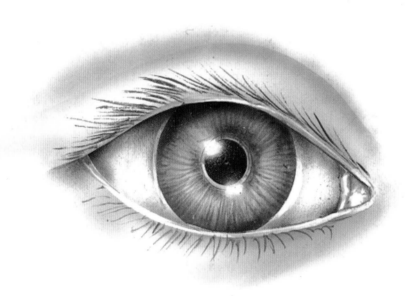

CONTENTS

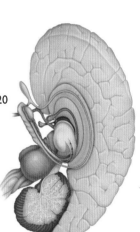

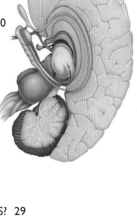

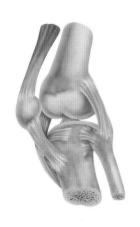

WHY IS OUR BLOOD RED?

Our blood is red because of the substance, haemoglobin, which is contained in our red blood cells (red corpuscles). The function of these specialised cells is to carry oxygen from our lungs to wherever it is needed in the body. They are formed in our bone marrow and the haemoglobin in them, which is made of iron and protein, becomes redder as it picks up oxygen. It loses this colour as it deposits oxygen in other cells and picks up carbon dioxide to carry back to the lungs, which is why some of the blood vessels in our hands and arms appear blue through our skin.

As well as carrying oxygen and carbon dioxide, the blood carries nutrients to the cells, so that they can perform their functions, and for cell repair and growth. Waste products are carried back to the liver for removal.

As well as the red cells, our blood also carries white blood cells, which help to fight off disease. All of the cells and nutrients are carried in a pale yellow, thick liquid which is called plasma. The other materials carried in the plasma include a substance called fibrinogen, which helps the blood to clot when we cut ourselves.

vein

heart

A network of blood vessels

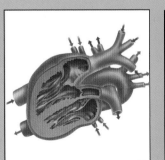

FACT FILE

Heart rate is the number of times that the heart actually contracts in a minute. You can measure this yourself by finding the pulse in your wrist, then gently holding your finger on it and counting the number of beats per minute.

WHY ARE ARTERIES DIFFERENT FROM VEINS?

There is no transportation system in any city that can compare in efficiency with the circulatory system of our body. If you can imagine two systems of pipes, one large and one small, both meeting at a central pumping station, you will have an idea of the circulatory system. The smaller pipes go from the heart to the lungs and back, while the larger ones go from the heart to the various other parts of the body. These pipes are called arteries, veins and capillaries.

artery

Arteries are vessels in which blood is carried away from the heart. In veins, the blood is coming back to the heart. In general terms, arteries are carrying pure blood to various parts of the body, and the veins are bringing back blood loaded with waste products. The pumping station is of course the heart.

Arteries lie deep in the tissues, except at the wrist, over the instep, at the temple and along the sides of the neck. At any of these places the pulse can be felt, which gives the doctor an idea of the condition of the arteries. The blood in arteries is bright red in colour and moves through in spurts.

Veins lie closer to the surface of the skin, and the blood in them is much darker in colour and flows more evenly. Veins have valves at intervals all along their course.

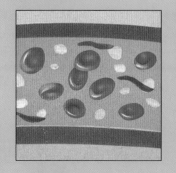

FACT FILE

Blood contains red and white blood cells that float inside a liquid called plasma. It also contains thousands of different substances needed by the body. Blood carries all these things round the body and also removes waste products.

WHY DO WE HAVE A SKELETON?

A skeleton is made up of a network of bones. Bones provide a framework that holds the whole body together.

Without a skeleton we would not be supported and would simply flop about like a rag doll. This would mean that we would not be able to move about.

The skeleton also gives protection to delicate organs in our bodies such as the brain, heart and lungs. It acts as a support to all the soft parts of the body.

The skeleton also provides a system of levers that the muscles can work on, enabling us to carry out all our movements.

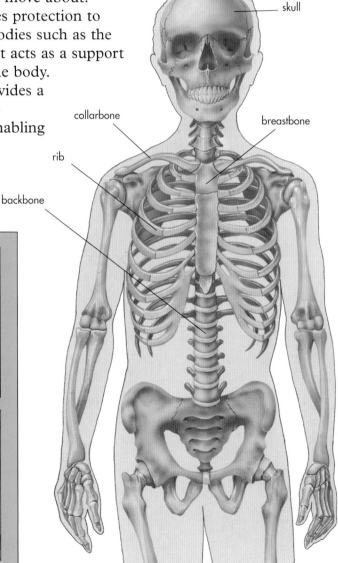

skull

collarbone

breastbone

rib

backbone

FACT FILE

At birth a baby has 300 bones, but 94 join together in early childhood. Your hand and wrist alone contain 27 bones.

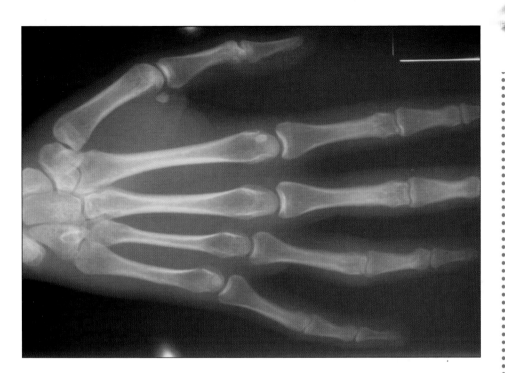

WHY DO PEOPLE HAVE X-RAYS TAKEN?

If we have an accident, often we go to hospital to have an X-ray taken of our body to see if we have any broken bones. The X-ray 'picture' is a shadowgraph or shadow picture. X-rays pass through the part of the body being X-rayed and cast shadows on the film. The film is coated with a sensitive emulsion on both sides. After it is exposed, it is developed like ordinary photographic film. The X-ray does not pass through bones and other objects so it casts denser shadows which show up as light areas on the film. This will show the doctor whether any bone has been broken or dislocated.

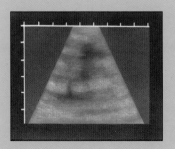

FACT FILE

Like X-rays, ultrasonic sound waves travel into the body and are bounced back by the organs inside. A screen can display the reflected sound as a picture. This is used to scan an unborn baby in the mother's womb.

WHY IS WATER GOOD FOR US?

Water is absolutely essential to every single form of life. Every living cell – plants and animals alike – depend on this substance.

More than half of the human body is made up of water. Much the same is true of other living things. Without water to drink, human beings would die in a very short time.

The reason every living thing needs a certain amount of water is because the cells, the basic units that make up living things, have water molecules in them. Without water these basic units would be very different and of no use to life as we know it.

In the course of a day, an adult human being takes in about two quarts of water as fluids, and one quart in what we call solid foods, such as fruit, vegetables, bread, and meat. These solid foods are not really dry, since they are thirty to ninety percent water.

Besides these three quarts that enter the body from outside, about ten quarts of water pass back and forth within the body between the various organ systems.

There are about five quarts of blood in the vessels of the body and three quarts of this is water. And this always remains unchanged. No matter how much water you drink you cannot dilute the blood.

FACT FILE

Our sense of thirst is controlled in the brain. When the body requires more water, we experience the sensation of thirst. Usually our mouth and throat become dry – a signal for us to drink more fluids.

WHY ARE CELLS IMPORTANT?

mitochondria

cell membrane

cytoplasm

nucleus

Cross-section of an animal cell

Apart from water the rest of the body is built from a huge number of complicated chemicals. These chemicals, together with water, are assembled into tiny building blocks called cells. Each cell is self-contained and has a particular function in the body. There are more than 50,000 billion cells in your body. The shape and appearance of a cell depends on what type of job it has to do. Nerve cells are long and thread-like and can carry messages around the body along the nervous system. Red blood cells are so tiny that they can only be seen under a microscope and are like flattened discs. The sole function of the blood cell is to combine with oxygen in the lungs and to exchange the oxygen for carbon dioxide in the tissues. White blood cells are shapeless so they can squeeze between other cells and attack invaders such as bacteria. Other cells control the production of essential substances called proteins.

FACT FILE

Metabolism is the term for all of the chemical activity that takes place inside the cells. Metabolism breaks down more complicated substances obtained from food. Our metabolic rate rises during vigorous exercise.

WHY DO PEOPLE GET ALLERGIES?

An allergy is any condition in which a person reacts in a hyper-sensitive or unusual manner to any substance or agent. The range of allergies is very broad and people may react to various foods, drugs, dusts, pollens, fabrics, plants, bacteria, animals, heat, sunlight and many other things.

Whenever a foreign material invades the tissues, the body reacts to fight against it. The body produces certain materials called antibodies which combine with the foreign material and render it harmless. But should it enter the body a second time, the antibodies are torn away from the body tissues to attack the substance. This causes a chemical substance called histamine to be released, which in turn produce the disorders which are symptoms of an allergy.

FACT FILE

In spring and early summer some people suffer from an allergic reaction to certain plants and pollens. This is called hay fever and can give the symptoms of a heavy cold.

WHY DO SOME PEOPLE GET ASTHMA?

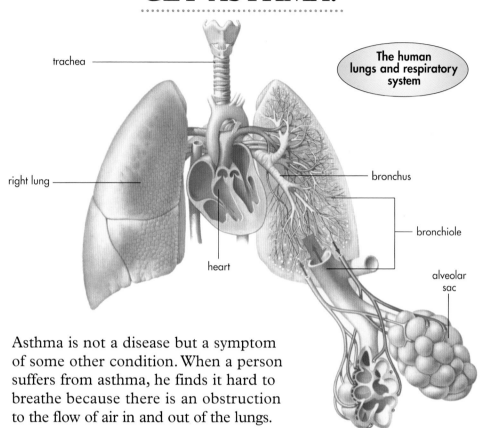

trachea

right lung

heart

The human lungs and respiratory system

bronchus

bronchiole

alveolar sac

Asthma is not a disease but a symptom of some other condition. When a person suffers from asthma, he finds it hard to breathe because there is an obstruction to the flow of air in and out of the lungs.

The cause may be an allergy, an emotional disturbance, or atmospheric conditions. If a person develops asthma before he is 30 years old, it is usually the result of an allergy. He may be sensitive to pollens, dust, animals, or certain foods or medicines.

Children, especially, tend to develop asthma from food allergies. These are often caused by eggs, milk, or wheat products. People who have asthma are often put on special diets to eliminate or minimise contact with these food products.

FACT FILE

People can develop allergies to many different foods. One of the most common is to dairy related products.

WHY DO WE OFTEN LOOK LIKE OUR PARENTS?

The characteristics of individual human beings are passed from one generation to the next in their chromosomes. Each of our parents gives us 23 chromosomes, making 46 in all. That means that we have two versions of each of our genes, but one is often dominant. We see the effect of the dominant gene, but the other (recessive) gene is still there and can be passed on to our children.

Chromosomes are tiny threads that are present in all cells apart from the red blood cells. They contain all the information for an entire person to develop. There is a special pair that actually determine's a person's sex.

Short sections of a chromosome are called genes. Each gene carries the instructions for a specific characteristic, such as an eye colour. Many of these genes work with other genes, so it is not easy to say what effects they will have. Scientists are currently studying all the genes in a human cell, which will give them the complete blueprint for a human being.

FACT FILE

The gene for brown eyes is the dominant gene. Two brown eye genes give brown eyes, one brown gene and blue gene usually give brown eyes. Two blue eye genes give blue eyes.

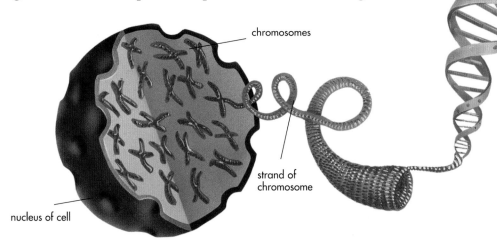

chromosomes

strand of chromosome

nucleus of cell

WHY DO WE HAVE CHROMOSOMES?

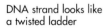

How a DNA molecule is formed

Every cell has a nucleus which is full of information coded in the form of a chemical called deoxyribonucleic acid (or DNA). The DNA is organized into groups called genes. Every chromosome contains thousands of genes, each with enough information for the production of one protein. This protein may have a small effect within the cell and on the appearance of the body. It may make all the difference between a person having brown or blue eyes, straight or curly hair, normal or albino skin.

At the moment the mother's egg is fertilized, the genes start issuing instructions for the moulding of a new human being. Every characteristic which we inherit from our parents is passed on to us through the coding of the genes within the chromosomes.

In rare cases, some people have 47 chromosomes. This occurs when people inherit Downs Syndrome, a genetic disorder.

rings of pairs of amino acids

DNA strand looks like a twisted ladder

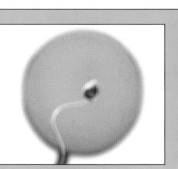

FACT FILE

A baby starts when two special cells meet – a sperm cell from a man's body and an egg cell from a woman's body. Joined inside the woman's body, these two cells grow into a whole new person.

WHY IS EXERCISE GOOD FOR US?

Regular exercise is important because it keeps bones, joints and muscles healthy. During any physical exertion, the rate at which the heart beats increases, as it pumps more oxygenated blood around the body. How quickly the heart rate returns to normal after exercise is one way to assess how fit someone is and how exercise is actually improving their fitness.

Once almost everyone did manual work of some kind. It was essential for survival. Human bodies were not designed for the inactive lives many of us now lead. That is why exercise is important for good health.

FACT FILE

Swimming is a very good form of exercise as it uses lots of muscles without causing strain.

WHY DO MUSCLES ACHE AFTER EXERCISE?

When you exercise your muscles contract and produce an acid known as lactic acid. This acid acts like a 'poison'. The effect of this lactic acid is to make you tired, by making muscles feel tired. If the acid is removed from a tired muscle, it stops feeling tired and can go right to work again.

So feeling tired after muscular exercise is really the result of a kind of internal 'poisoning' that goes on in the body. But the body needs this feeling of tiredness so that it will want to rest. During rest the joints of the body replace the supplies of lubricants they have used up.

TELL ME WHY : THE HUMAN BODY

WHY DO WE STOP GROWING?

The average baby is about one foot, eight inches long at birth. Over the next twenty years, man triples the length of the body he was born with and reaches an average height of about five feet, eight inches. But why doesn't he just keep on growing and growing?

In the body there is a system of glands called the endocrine glands which control our growth. The endocrine glands are: the thyroid in the neck, the pituitary attached to the brain, the thymus which is in the chest and the sex glands. The pituitary gland is the one that stimulates our bones to grow. If this works too hard our arms and legs would grow too long and our hands and feet too big. If the gland doesn't work hard enough, we would end up as midgets.

We continue to grow, but only slightly, after the age of 25, and we reach our maximum height at about the age of 35 or 40. After that, we shrink about half an inch every ten years. The reason for this is the drying-up of the cartilages in our joints and in the spinal column as we get older.

FACT FILE

Older people are no longer growing and so they are not as active as they used to be. For this reason they do not need to eat as much and quite often become thinner.

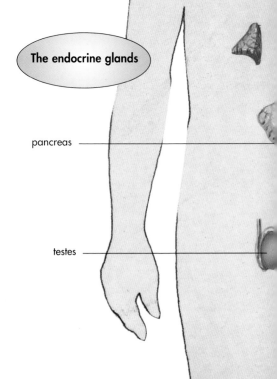

The endocrine glands

pancreas

testes

WHY DON'T WOMEN HAVE BEARDS?

We know that beautiful hair in a woman can be very attractive, but we must assume that hair on human beings formerly played a more practical role than it does now. When a baby is born he is covered with a fine down. This is soon replaced by the delicate hair which we notice in all children. Then comes the age of puberty, and this coat of fine hair is transformed into the final coat of hair which the person will have as an adult.

pituitary

thyroid

The development of this adult hair is regulated by the sex glands. The male sex hormone works in such a way that the beard and body hair are developed, while the growth of the hair on the head is inhibited, or slowed down in development.

The action of the female sex hormone is exactly the opposite! The growth of the hair on the head is developed, while the growth of the beard and body hair is inhibited, so women don't have beards because various glands and hormones in their bodies deliberately act to prevent this growth.

adrenals

FACT FILE

The custom of shaving was introduced to England by the Saxons. Barbers first appeared in Roman times in 300BC. Nowadays, there is a great variety of facial hair-styles from beards and moustaches to the clean-shaven effect.

FACT FILE

Vitamin C is an essential vitamin which helps to fight off infections and illnesses. This can be found naturally in oranges and other fruit and vegetables so it is very important that we include plenty of these in our everyday diet.

WHY DOES OUR TEMPERATURE RISE WHEN WE'RE ILL?

The first thing your doctor will do when you don't feel well is to take your temperature with a thermometer. He is trying to find out whether you have a 'fever'.

Your body has an average temperature of 98.6 degrees fahrenheit when it is healthy. Some diseases make this temperature rise and we call this higher temperature 'fever'.

Fever actually helps us fight off sickness. Fever makes the vital processes and organs in the body work faster. The body produces more hormones, enzymes and blood cells. The hormones and enzymes are useful chemicals in our body and when we are ill will have to work much harder. Our blood circulates faster, we breathe faster and so we get rid of wastes and poisons in our system. It is important however to get rid of the fever as quickly as possible as it destroys vital protein in your body.

FACT FILE

The food we take in is fuel which the body burns up. In this process, about 2,500 calories are being used every day in the body.

WHY IS THE BODY WARM?

In order for the body to carry on its functions efficiently it needs energy. This energy is obtained through a process called combustion. The fuel for their combustion is the food that we take in. The result of combustion in the body is not, of course, a fire or enormous heat. It is a mild, exactly regulated warmth. There are substances in the body whose job it is to combine oxygen with the fuel in an orderly, controlled way.

The body maintains an average temperature regardless of what is going on outside. This is done by the centre in the brain known as the temperature centre, which really consists of three parts: a control centre which regulates the temperature of the blood, one that raises the temperature of the blood when it drops, and a third that cools the blood when the temperature is too high.

When we shiver it is the body's automatic reaction to the temperature of our blood dropping too low. Shivering actually produces heat!

WHY DO WE TAKE ANTIBIOTICS?

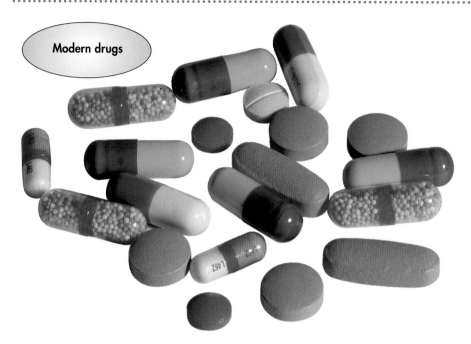

Modern drugs

Antibiotics are chemicals. When these chemicals are put into the body they kill or stop the growth of certain kinds of germs. In other words they help your body to fight off disease.

Many modern antibiotics are made from microbes, which are tiny living things. For example, bacteria and moulds are microbes. The microbes used in making antibiotics are chosen for their ability to produce chemicals that wage war on the microbes of disease. In simple terms this means that man is taking advantage of the struggle that goes on in nature among microbes.

Antibiotics are very effective at curing diseases and work in various ways. One antibiotic may act in different ways against different germs. It may kill the germs in one case and in another only weaken them and let the body's natural defences take over.

FACT FILE

Today a lot of people are turning to natural remedies rather than prescribed drugs. These are made from natural products like roots, plants, flowers and trees.

WHY ARE VIRUSES DIFFERENT FROM BACTERIA?

Both bacteria and viruses are the most important causes of disease. Bacteria are simple plant-like organisms that can divide very quickly. They cause many common infections such as boils and acne.

Viruses are very much smaller and technically they are not alive at all. They can take over the functioning of an infected cell and turn it into a factory producing millions more viruses. Viruses are responsible for many common diseases such as colds and influenza.

The diagram below shows us how a virus invades a cell: (1) they shed their outer layer (2) and take over the genetic material in the host cell in order to reproduce themselves (3). They begin to construct protein coats around the new viruses (4) and eventually burst out of the host cell (5) to leave it in an envelope (6) ready to infect new cells.

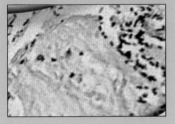

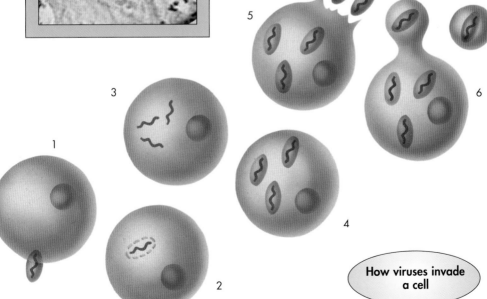

How viruses invade a cell

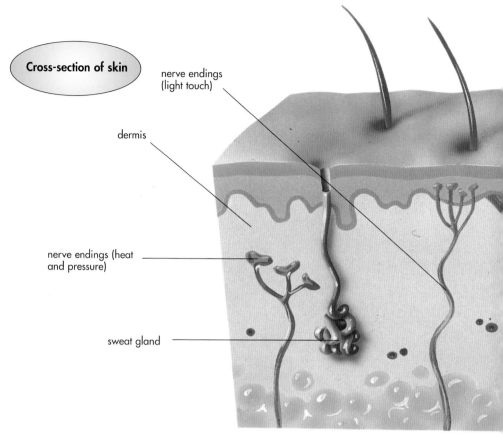

Cross-section of skin

nerve endings
(light touch)

dermis

nerve endings (heat
and pressure)

sweat gland

WHY DO WE HAVE SKIN?

Skin is a flexible, waterproof covering that protects us from the
outside world. It prevents harmful germs from entering the body.
Skin is your largest organ and it is sensitive to touch, temperature
and pain. Your skin tells you what is happening around your body,
so you can avoid injuring yourself. It also helps to prevent damage
from the Sun's harmful ultraviolet rays. Finally skin helps to
regulate body temperature by sweating and flushing to lose heat
when you get too hot.

FACT FILE

Over time, the appearance of skin changes: it
becomes more wrinkled and creased. As people
age, the collagen fibres in their skin weaken,
causing the skin to become looser.

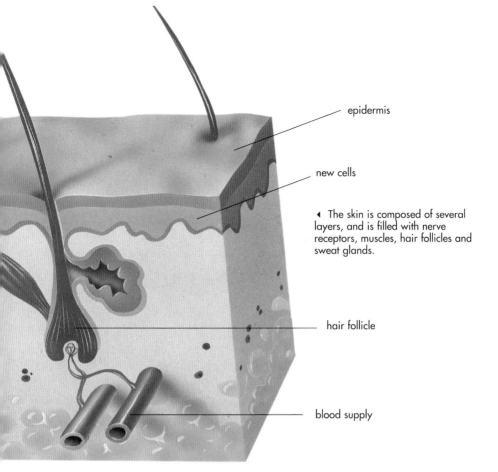

epidermis

new cells

◄ The skin is composed of several layers, and is filled with nerve receptors, muscles, hair follicles and sweat glands.

hair follicle

blood supply

WHY DO WE PERSPIRE?

FACT FILE

Perspiration is the body's own way of cooling down quickly. When a liquid evaporates it takes heat from wherever it is located.

Perspiration is one of the ways we keep our body at a nice normal temperature, around 98.6 degrees fahrenheit. When we become too hot the vessels in the skin are opened so that the extra heat can radiate away and also to help our perspiration to evaporate. Perspiration is like a shower which washes the body out from within. The fluid flows out through millions of tiny openings in the skin in the form of microscopic drops. These drops evaporate quickly and cool the body when necessary.

WHY DO WE DREAM?

All our dreams have something to do with our emotions, fears, longings, wishes, needs and memories. But something on the 'outside' may influence what we dream. If a person is hungry, tired, or cold, his dreams may well include these feelings. If the covers have slipped off your bed, you may dream you are on an iceberg. There are people called psychoanalysts who have made a special study of why people dream. They believe that dreams are expressions of wishes that didn't come true. In other words, a dream is a way of having your wish fulfilled. During sleep, according to this theory, our inhibitions are also asleep.

FACT FILE

Daydreaming is actually a form of dreaming, only it is done while we are awake. Night dreaming is done while we are asleep. That is the only difference between them, since both are done when the dreamer is so relaxed that he pays no attention to what goes on around him.

WHY DO WE AWAKEN FROM SLEEP?

Everybody has strange experiences with sleep. Sometimes we can't wait to go to sleep and other times we just can't seem to get to sleep. What actually wakes us up is something that scientists find hard to explain. When we go about thinking and seeing and feeling and carrying on mental activities of all sorts, we use up a lot of energy. So the brain and other nerve centres need a rest. Sleep clears away our tiredness and when we wake up we feel rested. The most probable reason is that while we are asleep our body still feels hungry, cold or even damp, or we may experience an emotion such as fear. These feelings stimulate our brain and cause us to wake up. Of course we may wake up simply because we have had enough sleep!

FACT FILE

Even while the body sleeps, its nerve systems are active, continuously monitoring and adjusting the internal processes, and checking the outside world for danger. The heart never stops, but beats slower while at rest.

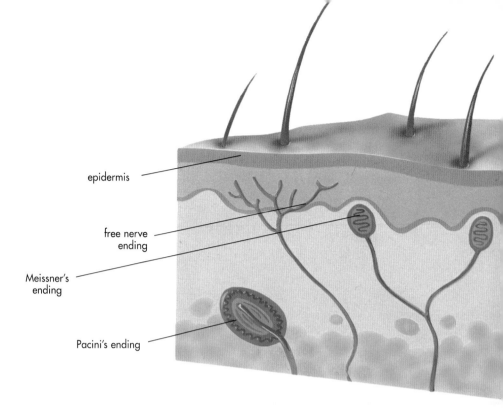

epidermis

free nerve
ending

Meissner's
ending

Pacini's ending

WHY IS TOUCH AN IMPORTANT SENSE?

Your skin is continuously passing huge amounts of information to your brain. It monitors touch, pain, temperature and other factors that tell the brain exactly how the body is being affected by its environment. Without this constant flow of information you would keep injuring yourself accidentally. You would be unable to sense whether something was very hot, very cold, very sharp and so on. In some rare diseases the skin senses are lost and these people have to be very careful so that they don't keep hurting themselves.

FACT FILE

Did you ever wonder why someone was called a 'touch typist'? This means that they are able to operate typewriter keys without actually looking at them.

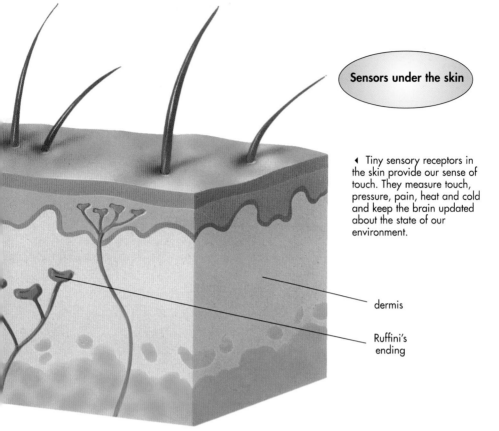

◄ Tiny sensory receptors in the skin provide our sense of touch. They measure touch, pressure, pain, heat and cold and keep the brain updated about the state of our environment.

dermis

Ruffini's ending

WHY ARE SOME BODY PARTS MORE SENSITIVE THAN OTHERS?

FACT FILE

The hands are among the body's most sensitive parts. The fingertips are especially sensitive. On one hand there are millions of nerve-endings.

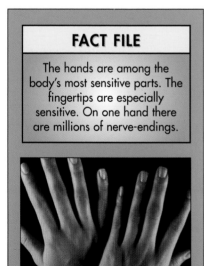

Sensations in the skin are measured by tiny receptors at the ends of nerve fibres. There are several different types of receptor. Each type can detect only one kind of sensation, such as pain, temperature, pressure, touch and so on. These receptors are grouped together according to the importance of their function. There are large numbers in the hands and lips, for example, where the sensation of touch is very important. Your back, however, is far less sensitive as there are fewer receptors in that area of your body.

29

WHY DO WE GET THIRSTY?

All of us have had the experience of being thirsty at times, but can you imagine how it would feel to be thirsty for days? If a human being has absolutely nothing to drink for five to six days, he will die. Feeling thirsty is simply our body's way of telling us to replenish its liquid supply.

The reason for this thirst is caused by a change in the salt content of our blood. There is a certain normal amount of salt and water in our blood. When this changes by having more salt in relation to water in our blood, thirst results.

There is a part of our brain called the 'thirst centre'. It responds to the amount of salt in our blood. When there is a change, it sends messages to the back of the throat. From there, messages go to the brain, and it is this combination of feelings that makes us say we are thirsty.

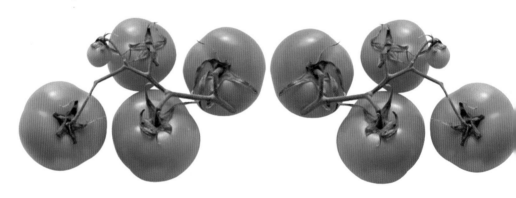

FACT FILE

Onions send out an irritating substance when we peel them. The onion has an oil containing sulphur which not only gives it its sharp odour, but it also irritates the eye. The eye reacts by blinking and producing tears to wash it away. That is why we cry when we peel onions.

WHY DO WE GET HUNGRY?

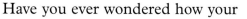

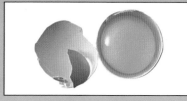

Have you ever wondered how your brain gets the message that makes us feel hungry? Hunger has nothing to do with an empty stomach, as most people believe.

Hunger begins when certain nutritive materials are missing in the blood. When the blood vessels lack these materials, a message is sent to a part of the brain that is called the 'hunger centre'. This hunger centre works like a brake on the stomach and the intestine. As long as the blood has sufficient food, the hunger centre slows up the action of the stomach and the intestine. When the food is missing from the blood, the hunger centre makes the stomach and intestine more active. That is why a hungry person often hears his stomach rumbling.

When we are hungry, our body doesn't crave any special kind of food it just wants nourishment. It depends on the individual how long we can actually live without food. A very calm person can live longer than an excitable one because the protein stored up in his body is used up more slowly.

FACT FILE

Eggs are an extremely good form of protein, which is vital for the building up and repair of muscles. Milk and dairy products are another good source of protein.

WHY ARE SOME PEOPLE LEFT-HANDED?

About four per cent of the population is left-handed. In the course of history many of the greatest geniuses have also been left-handed. Leonardo da Vinci and Michelangelo, the greatest sculptors of all times, were both left-handed.

The brain has a right half and a left half and these two do not function in the same way. It is believed that the left half of the brain is predominant over the right half.

As the left half of the brain predominates, the right half of the body is more skilled and better able to do things. We read, write, speak, and work with the left half of our brain. And this, of course, makes most of us right-handed too. But in the case of left-handed people, it works the other way around. The right half of the brain is predominant, and such a person works best with the left side of his body.

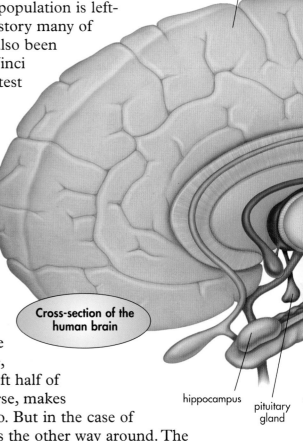

cerebrum

Cross-section of the human brain

hippocampus

pituitary gland

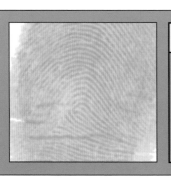

FACT FILE

Did you know that no two human beings have the same set of fingerprints? A fingerprint is the pattern formed by the ridges on the layers of skin at the tips of your fingers. If you press your finger on an ink pad and then onto a piece of paper, you should be able to see some of these patterns.

WHY CAN WE BALANCE ON TWO LEGS?

thalamus

Just being able to stand up or to walk is one of the most amazing tricks it is possible to learn. When you stand still you are performing a constant act of balancing. You change from one leg to the other, you use pressure on your joints, and your muscles tell your body to go this way and that way. Just to keep our balance as we stand still takes the work of about 300 muscles in our body. In walking, we not only use our balancing trick, but we also make use of two natural forces to help us. The first is air pressure. Our thigh bone fits into the socket of the hip joint so snugly that it forms a kind of vacuum. The air pressure on our legs helps keep it there securely. This air pressure also makes the leg hang from the body as if it had very little weight. The second natural force we use in walking is the pull of the Earth's gravity. When we raise our leg, the Earth pulls it down again.

brain stem

cerebellum

spinal cord

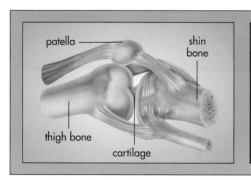

patella

shin bone

thigh bone

cartilage

FACT FILE

The knee joint, like your elbow, is a hinge joint. The end of one bone fits into a sort of hollow in the other. This kind of joint will only bend in one direction.

WHY DO WE NEED VITAMIN C?

The food we take into our bodies supplies us with many important substances such as proteins, fats, carbohydrates, water and mineral substances. But these alone are not enough. In order to maintain life we need other substances known as vitamins. Vitamin C can be found in citrus fruits and fresh vegetables. When there is a lack of vitamins in our body, diseases will occur. So what actually happens when there is a lack of this vitamin in the body? The blood vessels become fragile and bleed easily. Black-and-blue marks appear on the skin and near the eyes. The gums bleed easily. Our hormones and enzymes do not function well and our resistance to infection by bacteria is lowered.

Long before man knew about vitamins, it had been observed that when people couldn't get certain types of foods, diseases would develop. Sailors, for instance, who went on long trips and couldn't get fresh vegetables, would develop a disease called scurvy. In the seventeenth century British sailors were given lemons and limes to prevent this disease.

FACT FILE

Fruits contain energy and a wide range of essential vitamins and minerals. Vitamins are chemicals that we need to stay healthy. Some are stored in the body, others need to be eaten every day.

WHY ARE CARBOHYDRATES IMPORTANT?

Human beings need a certain amount of food each day to supply them with energy. Almost all foods can supply some energy, but carbohydrates give us the most. Carbohydrates include foods like bread, cereal, potatoes, rice, pasta.

Our bodies have other requirements as well. In order to make sure that we are taking in everything we need, we should eat a wide variety of foods, with the correct amounts of carbohydrates, fat and protein. A diet which fulfils these requirements is called a balanced diet.

These food groups serve different purposes: carbohydrates for energy, protein to build and repair cells and to keep our bones, muscles, blood and skin healthy.

FACT FILE

Bananas are a very good source of energy as the body absorbs them very quickly. Ripe bananas give off a gas that causes other fruit to ripen rapidly and then rot.

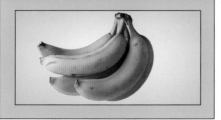

WHY DO SOME PEOPLE WEAR GLASSES?

If the eye is not exactly the right shape, or the lens cannot focus properly, you cannot form a clear image on the retina. In this case you may need to wear glasses to correct your vision. For a short-sighted person, distant object look blurred because the image forms in front of the retina. A short-sighted person can see nearby objects very clearly. For a long-sighted person, the image tries to form behind the retina, so it is blurred while the lens tries to focus on a nearby object. As people get older the lenses of their eyes grow harder and cannot change their shape to focus close up.

FACT FILE

Blinking is a very important function because it cleans and lubricates the surface of the eye. The cornea in particular is a sensitive area and must be protected from drying out and infection.

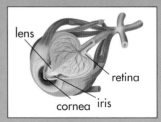

lens

retina

cornea iris

WHY DO WE SEE IN COLOUR?

The retina of the eye is packed with a layer of tiny cells called rods and cones. These cells contain coloured substances that react when light falls on them, triggering a nerve impulse. Rods are slim cells that are responsible for black and white vision. Cone cells give us colour vision. They contain different light-sensitive substances that respond to either red, yellow-green or blue-violet light. Together with the black and white images produced from the rods, cone cells give you the coloured picture that you see. The cone cells only work in bright light which is why it is difficult to see colours in a dim light.

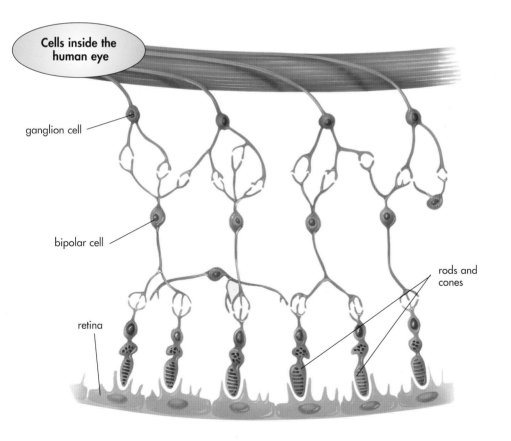

Cells inside the human eye

ganglion cell

bipolar cell

rods and cones

retina

37

THE NATURAL

WORLD

CONTENTS

WHY DO LIVING THINGS HAVE LATIN NAMES ?

Carl Linnaeus
(1707–1778)

Most plants and animals have popular names that can vary from place to place. So a name needed to be given that would be recognized everywhere. It was decided to use Latin for the scientific names, as it was the language used centuries ago by learned people. Carl Linnaeus was the man who established the modern scientific method for naming plants and animals.

Scientific names are in two parts. The first part is the generic name, which describes a group of related living things. The second name is the specific name, which applies only to that living thing. This specific name may describe the living thing, or it could include the name of the person who discovered it.

FACT FILE

The Latin name for a human is *Homo sapien*, meaning 'thinking man'. A fossil form of *Homo*, or man, is *Homo habillis* (tool-using man).

WHY IS CHARLES DARWIN REMEMBERED?

The English scientist Charles Darwin is remembered for his ideas about evolution after years of study and travelling on voyages of exploration. He discovered that many small islands had populations of unique creatures. Darwin was able to show how these creatures differed from their close relatives elsewhere. In the Galapagos Islands, for example, he found a unique range of animal life, due to their isolation from the mainland.

Charles Darwin
(1809–1882)

▼ The giant tortoise is just one of the animals that Charles Darwin discovered when he visited the Galapagos Islands.

FACT FILE

The giraffe is an example of how natural selection helps evolution. Their ancestors had longer than average necks so that they could reach more food.

WHY DO TREES HAVE BARK?

The outer layers of trees and woody shrubs are known as bark. Bark has a number of functions in protecting the tree: it gives added rigidity to the structure, insulates the delicate inner layers and helps to shield them from damage by insects and diseases. It also stops water evaporating: without it the cycle of water rising through the trunk and sugars passing down would not occur.

Bark needs to be able to allow the tree trunk to expand as it grows year by year and some trees, such as silver birch, as well as some pines and stringybark eucalaptus shed bits of their bark continually so that this can happen.

FACT FILE

The coconut is a large, hollow nut which grows on a palm tree. It contains a milky fluid which you can drink. The white lining is also edible and used in cooking. The coconut fibres on the outside of the shell are used for making coconut matting and sacking.

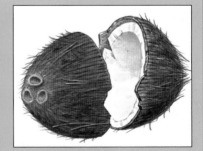

light energy from the Sun

water is taken in by the roots

WHY DO PLANTS HAVE ROOTS?

FACT FILE

Some plants, such as carrots and swede, are grown for their swollen edible taproots, which they use to store energy.

There are two main reasons: to provide stability and to obtain water and nutrients. There are two common types of root system: taproots, where the plant has one major root with others branching off from it and fibrous roots, where lots of smaller roots spread through the soil directly from the bottom of the plant's stem.

There are some plants that do not use their roots to obtain food, these include carnivorous plants, such as the venus fly trap, and 'epiphytic' plants that absorb nutrients through their leaves from the air, including the 'air plants' from South America.

WHY DO PLANTS PRODUCE SEEDS?

The seed of a plant contains an embryo from which a new plant will grow. It also contains a food store to nourish the embryo until it has developed roots and leaves. The seed is enclosed in a tough coat to protect it from drying out.

Many seeds are carried by the wind. Some, like the dandelion below, have fluffy 'umbrellas' which carry them for long distances. Others have wings that allow the seed to glide or spin around like a helicopter blade.

FACT FILE

The seed of the coco de mer can travel long distances by sea, until it is washed up onto shore. In the warm sand it sprouts and starts to grow into a new palm tree.

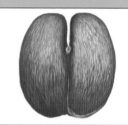

WHY DO TREES HAVE LEAVES?

The leaves are where most plants, including trees, manufacture their food. The substance that makes leaves green is called chlorophyll, which is contained in special cells called chloroplasts within them. The leaves are shaped and arranged to catch as much sunlight as possible because the chloroplasts use energy from the Sun to convert water and minerals from the soil and carbon dioxide from the air into sugars. This process is called photosynthesis (which means making from light).

FACT FILE

In the autumn many leaves change colour and drop from the tree. Because the tree does not grow in the winter, so it reabsorbs the green chlorophyll, and conserves its energy by losing its leaves.

WHY ARE THERE SO MANY FLOWER SHAPES?

The reason that flowers come in so many different shapes and colours is to help ensure that they are fertilized. Flowers that rely on insects for pollination must make sure that the insect is carrying pollen from the same kind of plant. The shape of the flower ensures that only certain kinds of insect can pollinate it. Flat flowers, such as daisies and sunflowers, can be visited by hoverflies and some bees. Flowers that are formed into tubes only attract insects that have long tongues.

FACT FILE

Bees are attracted to the colour and scent of a flower. They feed on the nectar in the flower and gather pollen, which they store in sacs on their legs.

WHY ARE SOME FLOWERS VERY COLOURFUL?

FACT FILE

Did you know that the bat's long tongue is perfect for whisking out the nectar from a flower? Pollen is brushed onto the bat's fur as it moves from flower to flower.

A flower is the means by which a plant reproduces. It contains male or female organs or both together. Flowers usually have brightly coloured petals or sepals.

The reason that flowers are so brightly coloured and perfumed is to attract insects. Insects play a very important part in pollinating them.

Some plants also produce a sugary liquid called nectar which attracts the bees. As they fly from flower to flower they transfer the pollen to the stigma of the flower and fertilize it.

TELL ME WHY : THE NATURAL WORLD

WHY ARE SPIDERS NOT INSECTS?

Spiders belong to the class of arachnids which also includes scorpions, ticks and mites. None of these are actually classed as insects. Unlike insects they have eight legs, eight eyes in most cases, no wings, and only two, not three parts to their bodies.

Spiders are found in practically every kind of climate. They can run on the ground, climb plants, run on water, and some even live in water.

The spider manufactures a silk, which it uses to spin its web, in certain glands found in the abdomen or belly. At the tip of the abdomen there are spinning organs which contain many tiny holes. The silk is forced through these tiny holes. When the silk comes out it is a liquid. As soon as it comes in contact with the air, it becomes solid. Spiders are meat-eaters, feeding on insects and other spiders which it traps in its web.

FACT FILE

The scorpion is related to the spider. A scorpion has four pairs of walking legs and a pair of strong pincers which it uses to grasp its prey. It also has a long, thin, jointed tail which ends in a curved, pointed stinger. This stinger is connected to poison glands.

WHY ARE SOME INSECTS BRIGHTLY COLOURED?

There are many different ways in which insects will try to protect themselves from their enemies. Some insects, such as wasps and ants, have powerful stings or are able to shower their attackers with poisonous fluid. The hoverfly does not sting, but its colouring is so like that of a wasp or bee that enemies are very wary of it. Other insects, such as stick insects, use camouflage. They look like the leaves and twigs among which they feed. The bright colouring on some insects warns its enemies that it may be poisonous.

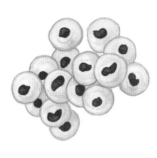

Frogspawn

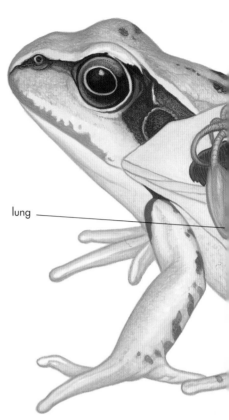

lung

▸ The internal organs of a frog are typical of vertebrate animals, although their lungs and heart are much simpler than those of mammals and birds.

WHY ARE SOME FROGS POISONOUS?

Not all frogs are poisonous but some have developed a venom that they can use should they come under attack from predators. The common toad contains a poison that it exudes through its skin if attacked. Dogs and cats commonly experience this poison, however they seldom suffer serious effects. It does teach them, however, to avoid these amphibians. Cane toads are very large toads which contain a drug capable of causing hallucinations if eaten. The skin of some frogs and toads contain poisons which are among the most powerful known to humans.

FACT FILE

The South American arrow frog is extremely poisonous. It advertises this danger by being very brightly coloured.

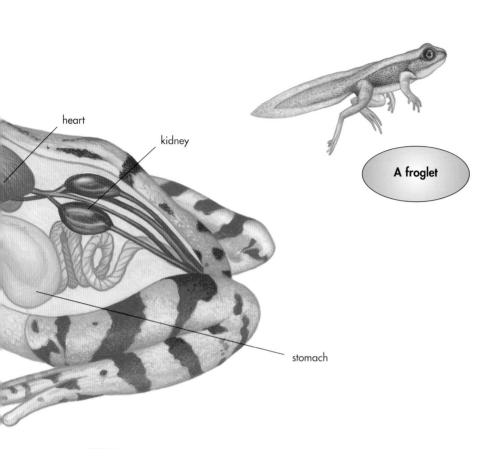

heart

kidney

stomach

A froglet

WHY DO FROGS VANISH IN WINTER?

Frogs vary considerably in shape, colour and size. Some little tree frogs, that live in the United States, are no more than one inch in length. Leopard frogs are about two to four inches long, while bullfrogs can reach eight inches and have legs that are ten inches long.

What do these frogs do in winter? In northern countries, when cold weather sets in, some frogs dive into a pond, bury themselves in the mud and stay there all winter. Ponds do not freeze solid, even when winters are very cold, so the frog does not freeze.

51

WHY DO SALMON GO UPSTREAM TO SPAWN?

Salmon have a natural instinct to return to the place they were born to lay their eggs (to spawn). This is a safe place, usually a quiet area of a river, where young salmon can grow. The adult salmon have fed at sea but stop eating when they reach fresh water, so most die of exhaustion after spawning. The eggs hatch after about two months, the young salmon stay near the hatchery for a few months, or even years, depending on the species, then make the journey down river to the sea. They will stay far out at sea for up to four years, before returning to the same river to breed.

FACT FILE

Adult frogs very often return to the pond in which they hatched to lay their spawn. Frog spawn hatches into larvae called tadpoles after about a week.

WHY CAN'T FISH SURVIVE OUTSIDE WATER?

Fish are specially adapted so that they can breathe under the water. They have special organs called gills. Gills are bars of tissue at each side of the fish's head. They carry masses of finger-like projections that contain tiny blood vessels. The fish gulp in water through their mouths and pass it out through the gills. The gills are rich in blood, and they extract oxygen from the water and pass it into the fish's blood.

In this way the gills have the same function as the lungs of air-breathing animals. But these gills would not work without the aid of water.

FACT FILE

Most of a fish's body is composed of powerful muscles and its internal organs are squeezed into a tiny area. The fins are used to propel and stabilize the fish in the water.

WHY DO BIRDS SING?

Male birds sing for two reasons: to attract mates in the breeding season and to warn other males to keep out of their territory.

Birds also use other calls to communicate with one another. When flying together, geese call to make sure that they stay in touch and adult penguins can recognise the voice of their own chick from among thousands in a colony.

Birds know instinctively how to sing but some species can learn to add new notes to their songs. Birds that are good at imitation, like starlings incorporate the sounds of car alarms in their songs and in Australia some superb lyrebirds have learned to imitate the noise of a chainsaw.

FACT FILE

If danger threatens her chicks, a hen will make a quiet noise that warns them to be still so that they do not attract attention.

WHY IS BIRDS' VISION SO GOOD?

Vision is the dominant sense of nearly all birds. In most, the eyes are placed so far to the side of the head that they have mainly monocular vision, meaning that each eye scans a separate area. This feature is shared by all hunted creatures who depend on vision to warn them of possible danger. Birds of prey and owls have eyes set more to the front of the head, offering a wider angle of binocular vision, which is vitally important for judging distance. Birds also have a third eyelid which moves sideways across the cornea and keeps it moist without interrupting their vision.

FACT FILE

Accuracy is crucial for a hunting bird like eagles which rely on their keen eyesight, first to spot the prey and then to catch it. Eagles' eyes are therefore positioned sufficiently far forwards to give them binocular or three-dimensional vision.

WHY DOES THE PEACOCK RAISE HIS FEATHERS?

The common peacock originates from India, but has been known in the West for thousands of years. The long train, which is not actually a tail, but is held up by the feathers of true tail beneath, is about half the total length of the male bird.

Only the males have trains; the females – peahens – are smaller, drab in colour and have smaller crests.

The male uses his beautiful plumage to impress females and in the breeding season will raise and quiver his train feathers in order to persuade them that he would make a good father for their chicks. They are mainly used as living garden ornaments in grand gardens and public parks.

Some peacocks and peahens are pure white. This is a colour mutation and in captivity selective breeding has been employed to produce this colour variation.

Peacock feathers have long been used in decorating hats, but in many areas it is thought bad luck to have them in the house.

FACT FILE

Ostrich eyes are nearly as big as tennis balls! Ostriches lay bigger eggs than any other bird – they are 24 times bigger than a chicken's egg. The shell is so strong that even if you stand on top of an ostrich egg, it will not break.

The male peacock

FACT FILE

The puffin's big, bright beak is hinged so that it can snap up fish and still keep a grip on those it has already caught.

WHY IS A MALE BIRD BRIGHTER THAN A FEMALE?

In many, but not all, bird species, the male has brighter plumage than the female and uses it to attract the female's attention and to see off rival males. Some birds also sing for the same purposes.

The female birds of most species do not need to display and are thought to have duller plumage because it makes it harder for predators to find them when they are sitting on the nest.

Not all birds keep their bright plumage all year round: male mallard ducks lose their bright green head feathers and their striking wing patterns after the breeding season. In puffins, the beak changes: after the breeding season, they lose the bright-coloured outer parts of the beak and regrow them for the following spring.

WHY DON'T SNAKES HAVE LEGS?

Just because snakes do not have legs now, does not mean they did not have them at sometime in their development. Some experts believe that the ancestors of snakes were certain kinds of burrowing lizards. In time, the legs disappeared altogether. Despite this snakes are able to move and get along very well indeed. One of the most helpful things for them in moving are the belly scales that cover the entire undersurface of most snakes. Snakes can move in different ways. The concertina method, which is used for climbing. Sidewinding, where a loop of the body is thrown to one side. The lateral undulatory movement, where the snake forms S-shaped curves, and also the rectilinear movement where it uses its scales.

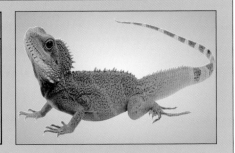

FACT FILE

Lizards and snakes belong to the highest order of reptiles. The main difference between lizards and snakes is in the structure of the jaws. In snakes, both upper and lower jaws have movable halves with sharp teeth.

WHY ARE CROCODILES NOT THE SAME AS ALLIGATORS?

Both crocodiles and alligators spend most of their lives in swamps and rivers in warm climates, although they breathe air through nostrils on the top of their snouts. They close these nostrils when they dive below the water. Caymans and gavials are relatives of crocodiles and alligators.

   The simple way of telling them apart is that crocodiles show the fourth tooth in their lower jaw when their mouths are closed. Alligators, on the other hand, do not. It is probably wise not to go near enough to a live crocodile to find out, however, as they have been known to attack humans.

FACT FILE

The Komodo dragon is a huge monitor lizard found living in Indonesia. This fearsome lizard is known to live for about 100 years. It can grow to a length of 3 metres.

An alligator

A crocodile

WHY DOES A GIRAFFE HAVE A LONG NECK?

FACT FILE

The elephant is also an unusual animal because of its very long trunk. It is an extension of the nose and upper lip and serves the elephant as hand, arm, nose and lips all at once.

Giraffes in the wild

The giraffe is the tallest of all living animals. The strange shape and build of the giraffe is perfectly suited to enable it to obtain its food. A giraffe only eats plants, so its great height enables it to reach the leaves on trees which grow in tropical lands where there is little grass.

A giraffe's tongue can be 18 inches (46cm) long and it uses it so skillfully that it can pick the smallest leaves off thorny plants without being pricked. It also has a long upper lip which helps it wrench off many leaves at a time.

If a giraffe wants to take a drink from the ground, it has to adopt a peculiar stance by spreading its legs far apart in order to be able to reach down.

WHY ARE RHINOS BECOMING ENDANGERED?

FACT FILE

The red wolf became extinct in the wild in 1980, but small numbers of captive specimens were bred. There are now around 200 in captivity.

Some animal species have become extinct because they are less successful than other species that gradually replace them. But this is not so in the case of the rhinoceros. Hunting is the reason for their reduced numbers. In fact poaching has reduced the numbers of black rhinos to around 2,500. Most survive today only in protected game parks. A rhino horn can grow as long as 62 inches (157cm).

WHY DOES A COW CHEW ITS CUD?

Many thousands of years ago, there were certain animals who couldn't protect themselves very well against their predators. In order to survive, these animals developed a special way of eating. They would snatch some food whenever they could, swallow it quickly without chewing, and run away to hide. When they were safe in their hiding place, they would chew the food at their leisure. Some present day animals, such as cows, still eat this way. It is called chewing the cud and the animals are called ruminants. This way of eating is possible because such animals have complicated stomachs with five compartments. Each of these compartments processes the food.

FACT FILE

Other examples of cud chewing animals are sheep, goats, camels, llamas, deer and antelopes. Camels find this form of eating very useful for long desert journeys.

WHY ARE BEARS DANGEROUS?

Bears can be up to 3 metres tall and usually have thick, shaggy coats. Bears actually look very cuddly, but they can be very fierce.

Bears are good tree climbers, powerful, quick to react, and relatively harmless to people except when provoked, cornered, or injured. Sometimes they can be a problem just through sheer friendliness.

In national parks, where they are familiar with human beings and come begging for food, visitors to the parks must keep to the protection of cars to avoid accidental injury from the bears' claws. Also with their big strong arms, bears could hug a person to death.

They are sometimes affectionately known as 'grizzly' bears. The reason for this is because the tips of their brown hairs are grey, or grizzled.

FACT FILE

Did you know that many bears have rotten teeth? This is because they love sweet foods. One of their favourite foods is honey which they steal from bees' nests high up in trees.

The American black bear

WHY IS THE LION CALLED 'KING OF THE BEASTS'?

Throughout history the lion has been considered the symbol of strength. In courts all over the world the lion was used on shields and crests and banners to indicate power. The lion's voice is a roar or a growl. The ancient Egyptians believed the lion was sacred, and during the time when Christ was born, lions lived in many parts of Europe. Today, the only places where lions are plentiful are in Africa.

FACT FILE

Lions and tigers are thought of as the greatest cats of the wild. Stripy tigers and lions never meet in the wild; lions are native to Africa, and stripy tigers are native to Asia.

WHY DO TIGERS HAVE DISTINCT COLOURING?

The tiger is one of the largest of the big cats. The base colour of the coat is fawn to red, becoming progressively darker the further southwards you go. The Balinese tiger is the darkest. The underparts of the tiger are white. The coat is overlaid with black to brownish-black transverse stripes and these contrasting colours provide a wonderful camouflage in its natural habitat.

FACT FILE

A leopard is another member of the big cat family which has a remarkable coat. Did you know that the name leopard is from the Latin word *leopardus* which means a 'spotted lion'?

WHY ARE SOME APES SO HUMANLIKE?

The great apes are the nearest living relative to man. There are four species of great ape: the orang-utan, chimpanzee, gorilla and the gibbon. Chimpanzees are particularly brainy and are one of the few animals to actually use tools. Apes generally walk on all fours but are able to stand and walk on two feet just like humans. Apes also have fingers and thumbs like a human hand, which makes them able to pick up and hold things as we do. The hair on an ape's head also turns grey with age as with humans. Baby gorillas, like human babies, learn to crawl at about ten weeks and walk at about eight months old.

FACT FILE

Apes like this gibbon give birth to helpless young that need looking after for a long time. Apes can look after their young for as long as five years.

WHY ARE MONKEYS DIFFERENT FROM OTHER PRIMATES?

All monkeys are primates. It is easy to tell them apart from the clever primates, people and apes, because they have tails. Their tails, which are generally long, can be used like an extra arm or leg to cling onto branches. A spider-monkey, from South America, can actually hang by its strong tail leaving both hands free for feeding. They live in family groups and spend much of their time in the trees. They are very careful to look around them before leaping from one tree to another as there could be danger close by. A large eagle may swoop from above or possibly a leopard could be lurking below so it is important not to lose their footing.

FACT FILE

Monkeys have a varied diet. They are not known for their fussy tastes and are omniverous by nature. They will eat a wide variety of food – from flowers, leaves and fruit to insects and small frogs.

WHY ARE RAIN FORESTS BEING CUT DOWN?

Tropical rainforests contain the most varied mixtures of animals and plants of any habitat on the Earth. They contain large and small predators and a bewildering variety of birds. All these animals are supported by huge numbers of trees that produce fruit to feed them and their prey all year round. Unfortunately though, man is destroying their natural habitat. Rainforests are being cut down at an alarming rate, nearly 90 per cent of rainforest have been destroyed. Both large commercial farming companies and individual farmers clear the forest to gain land to cultivate and graze animals. Secondly, trees have been felled to supply tropical hardwoods for furniture making and building.

FACT FILE

It is estimated that over two million different species of plant and animal thrive in the rainforests and many have been undiscovered by man. Their destruction is a serious threat to our planet.

WHY ARE MOST CORAL REEFS PROTECTED?

FACT FILE

A star fish is one of the many thousands of creatures that make their home among the coral reefs. The star fish moves around on thousands of tiny tube feet, or they can use them to grab their prey of shellfish.

Coral reefs are the marine equivalent of rainforests. They are homes to thousands of species of fish and invertebrates, all living in a complex balance which makes the reef system an extremely stable environment. That is until the intervention of man.

Marine biologists spend a lot of time studying the reef and valuable new discoveries are made all the time. There are a great number of threats to coral reefs. Work must be done quickly to protect them. Therefore the education of people throughout the world is necessary if coral reefs are to survive.

A kitten

WHY DO FLEAS LIVE ON CATS AND DOGS?

Fleas live on cats and dogs so that they can feed on their blood. The warm coat provides an ideal environment for the female flea to live and lay her eggs. The flea that parasitises cats and dogs can also live on humans.

Because the flea can jump so high and far in relation to its body size, it finds it very easy to move from one host animal to another.

It is especially important for young kittens to be kept free of fleas as they can become so badly infested that their blood becomes thin and they get anaemia which will make them weak and unhealthy and slow down their growth.

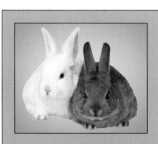

FACT FILE

Fleas don't just live on dogs and cats. They also infest rats, rabbits, squirrels, wild birds, and nearly all other warm-blooded animals.

WHY ARE SOME ANIMALS DOMESTICATED?

Dogs were probably the first animals to be domesticated, perhaps to help with hunting. By domesticating goats, cattle, sheep, pigs and poultry, humans have been able to ensure that food is always available. Horses, mules and camels have been used to carry people and goods over long distances. Pets provide companionship but can also be very useful. Sheepdogs help farmers to round up their flocks. Guide dogs for the blind and hearing dogs for the deaf help their owners to lead full lives. Animals are also used to guard property, perform rescues and carry messages.

The domesticated dog

SCIENCE AND

TECHNOLOGY

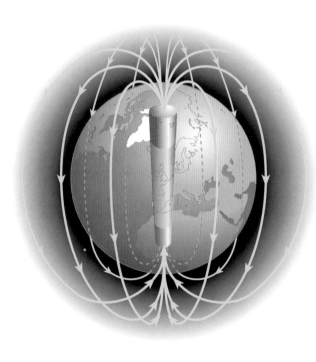

CONTENTS

WHY ARE ATOMS EVERYWHERE?

Atoms are the tiny particles that make up the whole universe. Enormous amounts of energy are locked inside atoms. Atoms are the tiniest particles into which a substance can be divided without changing into something else. Atoms actually consist almost entirely of open space, in which tiny particles orbit the central particle, or nucleus. The particles travel so fast that they seem to be solid.

Atoms are so minute that the smallest particle visible to the naked eye would contain about one million billion atoms. Despite their tiny size, atoms can be seen individually under very powerful electron microscopes.

Atoms linked to other atoms

FACT FILE

There are more than a hundred and nine different atoms. Atoms are so incredibly tiny – about 100,000 million atoms fit on this full stop.

atom.

WHY IS QUANTUM PHYSICS USED?

Quantum physics helps us to understand how energy is used or released by atoms. Negatively charged electrons circle about the positively charged nucleus of the atom. They stay in the same orbit until this is disturbed, and each orbit has its own lever of energy. If more energy is added when the atom is heated or when light shines on it, the electron jumps out to another orbit, absorbing the extra energy. Then when it drops back again to its original orbit, it releases this energy as heat or light. This tiny packet of energy is called a quantum. It is not possible to measure exactly where a subatomic particle is and how fast it is moving, because this will disturb the particle and change its characteristics.

FACT FILE

An atom becomes linked to other atoms by electrical bonds, which work rather like chemical hooks. Some atoms only carry one of these hooks, while others may have many. Atoms with many hooks can build up with other atoms into complicated molecules or chemical compounds.

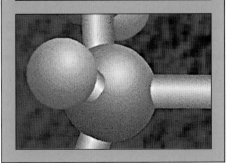

WHY ARE MICROSCOPES USED?

The word microscope is a combination of two Greek words, *mikros* or 'small' and *skopos* or 'watcher'. So this means that a microscope is a 'watcher of small' objects. It is an instrument that is used to see tiny things which are invisible to the naked eye.

Normally an object appears larger the closer it is brought to the human eye. But when it is nearer than 10 inches (25.5cm) it becomes blurred. It is said to be out of focus. Now if a simple convex lens is placed between the eye and the object, the object can be brought nearer than 10 inches (25.5cm) and still remain in focus. Today the microscope is important to man in almost every form of industry.

It was a Dutchman called Antonie van Leeuwenhoek (1632–1723) who discovered ground glass lenses which he used to examine the world about him. In the 1670s he made his first crude microscope with a tiny lens. This allowed him to be the first person to see microscopic life such as bacteria.

FACT FILE

Some microscopes are so powerful they can magnify the smallest objects many thousands of times. This plant cell would be invisible to the human eye without the use of magnification.

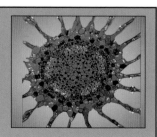

WHY IS PROTECTIVE CLOTHING WORN BY SCIENTISTS?

Two of the many things that scientists study are germs and bacteria that carry diseases. As many of these could be extremely dangerous if touched or sometimes just breathed in, it is essential for the scientist to wear protective clothing which would include masks, gloves, body and head protection.

Scientists sometimes have to handle radioactive material. Exposure to radioactive radiation can be fatal to any living organism. For this reason robots are used rather than human beings if at all possible. When people do need to handle such substances they wear protective clothing and carry a meter that records the amount of exposure to radiation they are receiving.

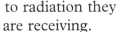

FACT FILE

This symbol on a container or buildings warns that there is some radioactive material inside.

neutral   acid   alkaline

WHY IS LITMUS PAPER USED IN CHEMISTRY?

Litmus paper is a quick way to test a liquid to see whether it is acid or alkaline.

Dyes called indicators show very quickly if a substance dissolved in water is acid or alkaline. One of these dyes is litmus. If a piece of paper impregnated with litmus is dipped into a solution, it immediately turns red if the solution is acid. If the solution is alkaline, the litmus turns blue.

A similar dye to litmus is present in some red vegetables, such as red cabbage and beetroot and this dye changes colour in the same way during cooking. If your tap water is hard, or alkaline, the vegetables will be coloured a deep purplish-blue.

FACT FILE

Bee stings are acidic. An acid is neutralized by an alkali, so as to reduce the painful effects of a bee sting. Soap is alkaline and will therefore help to lessen the effect of the sting if it is rubbed on the skin.

WHY ARE CRYSTALS FORMED?

Crystals are formed from dissolved substances, or when molten substances cool slowly. As the solutions evaporate or the melted materials cool, their atoms are forced closer together, producing a crystal. The crystal gradually grows as the process continues. Some crystals grow into complicated and beautiful shapes, which are often very brightly coloured.

Crystals are solid substances that have their atoms arranged in regular patterns. Most naturally occurring substances form crystals under the right conditions, although they are not always apparent.

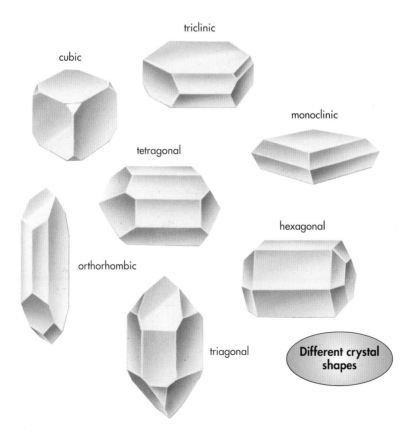

triclinic

cubic

monoclinic

tetragonal

hexagonal

orthorhombic

triagonal

Different crystal shapes

WHY DO WE USE CIRCUIT BOARDS?

Any modern electrical device requires a huge number of connections to join together all the small components needed for it to work effectively. At one time these connections were made by wires that had to be soldered together. The wires have now been replaced by the printed circuit board, which is effectively a picture of the wiring that works just as well.

The image is literally photographed onto a special board which is covered with a thin layer of copper. Chemicals are used to dissolve most of the copper leaving behind a thin film of metal bands to which all the components can be attached. Circuit boards are very light, compact and inexpensive to make.

FACT FILE

Appliances containing electronic circuits can perform very complicated tasks and even appear to think for themselves. A good example of this is a personal computer.

WHY DO WE SEE SO MANY PYLONS?

FACT FILE

In an electric light bulb an electrical current is passed through a very thin filament of metal. The filament becomes white hot and gives us light.

Electricity is used as a way of moving energy from place to place. It can take energy from burning coal in a power station into your home. Electricity is required for so many things in our homes and at our places of work that we need a way of getting the energy to travel. Giant masts called pylons have been erected all over the country which are connected by powerful electrical cables. Energy travels down these cables at about 250,000 kilometres a second, which is almost as fast as the speed of light.

WHY IS NUCLEAR POWER USED?

Inside a nuclear power station billions of uranium atoms are torn apart which create an enormous amount of energy. The energy is powerful enough to boil water, and steam from this hot water is used to generate electricity. Nuclear power holds out the promise of cheap and unlimited power, but with the technical difficulties and safety concerns their use is limited. The nuclear reactor at a power station is surrounded by thick concrete walls for safety.

FACT FILE

The atom bomb is such a powerful and dangerous weapon that it has only been used in anger twice. Even the testing of them has now been abandoned.

WHY ARE NUCLEAR REACTORS CONTINUALLY MONITORED?

People worry about nuclear power because when the energy is released from an atom, deadly rays, called radiation, can escape. Radiation is very harmful when it enters the body. When too much radiation passes through living cells, it may damage the cells or weaken the body's defences against disease. A typical nuclear power station produces about 20 bathfuls of dangerous waste each year. It is poured into steel tanks and are then buried in concrete.

FACT FILE

This is a nuclear reactor. Inside the reactor uranium or plutonium undergo a process called fission, which releases huge amounts of energy.

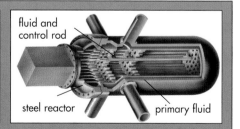

fluid and control rod

steel reactor

primary fluid

WHY ARE OPTIC FIBRES SO USEFUL?

An optical fibre is made of fine strands of glass, along which pulses of light can travel. Light travels much faster than electricity and it is therefore used in optical cables to carry communications for very long distances without electrical interference. The light travels along tiny glass fibres, usually packed into huge bundles capable of carrying many thousands of messages at the same time.

When you talk on the telephone your voice is turned into laser light signals and sent down very thin fibre glass tubes called optical fibres. Up to 150,000 different conversations can be sent down just one of these optical fibres.

Optic fibre is also used for ornate lighting. Light is reflected down thousands of tiny glass fibres as can be seen on some modern artificial Christmas trees.

FACT FILE

A great amount of communication these days is carried out via satellites. Radio, telephone and television messages are transmitted around the world with incredible speed. Such satellites orbit the Earth so that they appear to be in the same place all the time – even though the Earth is spinning round. This is possible because a satellite's orbit speed is matched with the Earth's rotational speed. These are known as geo-stationary orbits.

WHY ARE MEANS OF COMMUNICATION ALWAYS DEVELOPING?

light

glass fibre

Only a few hundred years ago, the fastest way a piece of news could travel was to be carried by a person on horseback. Messages sent overseas could only travel as fast as the fastest sailing ship. The breakthrough came with the invention of the electric telegraph and messages in Morse Code. The message was sent down a wire in bursts of electric current.

Today, however, images of written documents, sound recordings or television pictures can be flashed around the globe in less than a second by means of satellites and radio communications. Several satellites, in different orbits, are required to give coverage over the whole globe, and different satellites are used to reflect signals for different media, such as telephone messages and television pictures.

FACT FILE

Mobile phones work by using low-powered microwaves to send and receive messages to and from a base station. Otherwise known as a cellular phone, a mobile allows calls to be received and made wherever the caller happens to be.

WHY ARE WIND TURBINES USED AS A POWER SOURCE?

When oil, gas and coal run out, people will need other sources of energy to fuel their cars and light their houses. Concerns about pollution resulting from the production of electrical power have led to the development of wind turbines. Huge windmills situated on exposed and windy areas are a common sight in certain parts of the country.

Strong, steady winds can be put to work turning windmill blades. As the blades spin, they turn a shaft that generates electricity. These modern wind turbines come in several shapes. Large groups of them are called wind farms. The windmills of a wind farm can power generators to produce electricity for hundreds of homes.

FACT FILE

The principle of the windmill has been known since ancient times, but little is known of its use before the 12th century. They were used to pump water for livestock, household use, or for irrigation.

WHY ARE SOLAR PANELS ATTACHED TO ROOF TOPS?

There is always a constant search for new sources of energy. The Sun gives out vast amounts of energy, of which only a tiny fraction reaches the Earth. If we could use just a small part of this energy it would fulfil all the world's foreseeable needs for power. One way of harnessing the Sun's power is by using solar panels. Today a number of houses generate some of their own power. Solar panels attached to rooftops absorb the Sun's energy which is later used to heat domestic water supplies. The first solar power station was built in 1969 at Odeillo in France. It uses solar power to generate energy and has many solar panels to collect as much energy from the Sun as possible. One day scientists hope to collect sunlight in space and beam it back to Earth.

FACT FILE

The Sun's rays heat water in a pipe system within the solar panels. Cold water enters the pipes and flows through the panel, heating up as it goes. Hot water is collected from the pipes and stored for future use.

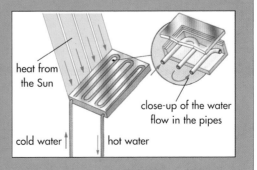

heat from the Sun

close-up of the water flow in the pipes

cold water ↑   hot water ↓

WHY DO SHIPS' NAVIGATORS RELY ON MICROWAVES?

Microwaves are a form of radiation. They can pass through things that would block ordinary radio waves, such as rain and fog. Microwaves can also be focused and sent in a narrow beam, making them very useful for transmitting radio messages over long distances.

Ships use these microwaves for navigation purposes. They have a radar screen which uses microwave radiation to detect distant objects. The microwaves usually scan round in a circle, and the echoes sent back produce an image on the screen.

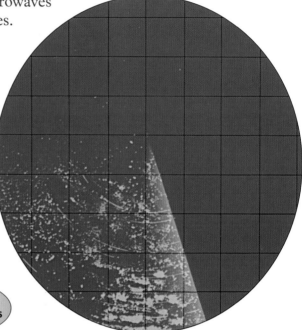

A radar screen using microwaves

FACT FILE

Air traffic controllers use the same system for keeping track of aircraft to pinpoint exactly where they are. It is important to see that planes are kept safely apart and are guided correctly during take-off and landing.

WHY DOES LIGHTNING FLASH?

As the atmosphere heats and cools, it expands and contracts, causing changes in pressure and air movement. Water droplets inside clouds have a positive electrical charge at the top of the cloud and a negative charge at the bottom. When the negative charge comes near enough to an attracting positive charge on the Earth below or on another cloud, the electrical energy is released in a flash of light. There may also be a loud bang, called thunder, at the same time. This is caused by the air being heated to a tremendous temperature, and the explosive noise is when it expands suddenly. However, as light travels faster through the air than sound, we see the lightning flash before hearing the thunder.

FACT FILE

Magnetic energy produced by vast storms on the Sun's surface strikes the upper atmosphere of the Earth, producing patterns in the sky near the poles called the Northern Lights or *aurora borealis*.

WHY DO WE NEED OIL?

Fossil fuels, which include oil, coal and natural gas, were formed millions of years ago when prehistoric plants and animals died. Their decaying bodies were pressed under layers of rock and earth and became fossilized. Life as we know it today would not be possible without fossil fuels. Not only are they burned to supply heat and energy to our homes and industry, but by forming the fuel for power stations, they also supply most of the electricity we use. Also fossil fuels can be processed to produce many other useful materials, including plastics, dyes and bitumen.

Geologists know what kinds of rocks are likely to contain or cover oil deposits. When they find a likely area on land or at sea, test drilling is carried out to find out if there is any oil beneath the surface.

drill

FACT FILE

Helicopters are an oilrig's lifeline. They not only bring workers food and supplies but they can also airlift a person to hospital should they have an accident or be taken ill.

WHY DO OIL RIGS SOMETIMES CATCH FIRE?

living quarters

platform

oil well

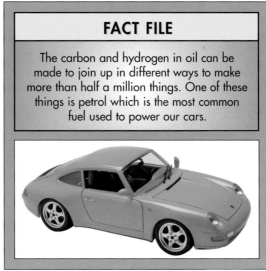

FACT FILE

The carbon and hydrogen in oil can be made to join up in different ways to make more than half a million things. One of these things is petrol which is the most common fuel used to power our cars.

Much of the world's oil is found buried beneath the seabed. Oil rigs are huge floating devices that are anchored to the seabed while wells are drilled into the oil-bearing rocks. These self-contained rigs contain all of the drilling machinery and a helicopter pad for receiving supplies.

When the oil is extracted from the rock it contains a large amount of gas which has to be burnt off at the surface. The gas gushing from an oil well can come out at great force and should this get ignited the resulting fire burns far too fiercely to be put out with water or normal fire extinguishers. Instead, firefighters use a special crane to position an explosive device in the flames. It may seem strange to fight a fire with an explosion, but when the explosion occurs, it takes the surrounding oxygen, temporarily depriving the fire and putting it out.

WHY IS STEEL AN IMPORTANT MATERIAL?

Iron has a lot of carbon in it which makes it crack very easily. If some carbon is removed, iron turns into super-strong steel. An enormous range of items can be made from steel, from tiny paperclips to huge girders forming the frames for skyscrapers. One very useful property of steel is that it can be recycled and used over and over again. Steel is the most important ingredient for making cars. Most screws, nails, nuts and bolts are made of steel and the huge cranes that make modern construction possible are built of steel. Also steel girders form the skeleton of new buildings.

FACT FILE

Stainless steel contains small amounts of nickel and chromium to make a metal that does not corrode. Many everyday things are made of stainless steel such as: cutlery, taps, sewing pins and needles and scissors.

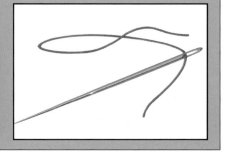

WHY ARE BLAST FURNACES USED?

Iron is the most widely used of all metals. It is cheap and very strong, so it can be used to make the supports for huge buildings and bridges. Smelting is what is known as a reduction reaction. It is a method of extracting iron from iron ore. The process of smelting takes place in something called a blast furnace, as pictured above. The blast furnace gets its name from the hot air that is blasted into it. This is where iron ore, limestone and coke (a form of carbon) are heated together while hot air is blasted into the furnace. The carbon in the coke reacts with the oxygen in the air to form carbon monoxide. This in turn takes oxygen from the iron ore, leaving behind iron mixed with a little carbon. The temperature inside the furnaces reaches 2000°C.

FACT FILE

Alloys of steel, in which steel is combined with other metals, can be very useful. Railway tracks are made of an alloy of steel and manganese.

WHY ARE THE WRIGHT BROTHERS REMEMBERED?

People had been flying in small airships, but there was a race on to make the first successful aeroplane. The Wright Brothers were the first people to invent a practical aeroplane that could be flown under full control. Their first flight took place in 1903 at Kitty Hawk in the United States.

The Wright biplane looked like a huge box kite, with a home-made engine that drove two propellers by means of chains. It was however a practical and successful aircraft as it flew and it was controllable, unlike an earlier steam-powered aeroplane flown in 1890 by Clément Adler in France.

FACT FILE

Frank Whittle designed the first true jet engine between 1928 and 1930, but it was not used to fly a jet aircraft until 1941. A German engineer, Hans von Ohain, began work on a similar jet engine in 1936. His engine had flown a Heinkel aircraft by the year 1939.

WHY IS HELICOPTER FLIGHT NOT A MODERN DISCOVERY?

FACT FILE

The hovercraft is an ingenious machine that rides on a cushion of air. It looks like a flat-bottomed ship and is powered by huge propellers.

Leonardo da Vinci (1452–1519) drew his plans for a helicopter hundreds of years before people were first able to fly. Helicopters are lifted into the air by their large rotating propellers or rotors. These work like narrow wings, generating lift as they spin rapidly through the air. It climbs by increasing the angle of the rotor blades. It moves forward by increasing the angle of the blade moving back on every rotation so that it pushes against the air.

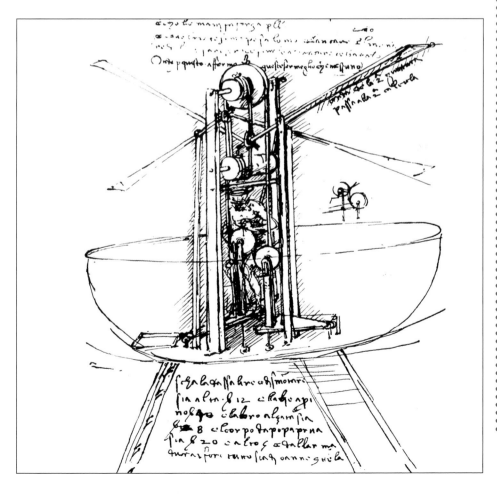

WHY ARE SUNDIALS USED?

The sun was man's first clock. Long ago men guessed at the time of day by watching the Sun as it moved across the sky. Then men noticed that the shadow changed length and moved during the day. They found they could tell the time more accurately by watching shadows than by looking at the Sun. From this it was an easy step to inventing the sundial. The first sundials were probably just poles stuck into the ground, with stones placed around the pole to mark the position of the shadow. Sundials have been in use for many centuries and are still in use today

A sundial

WHY DO WE NEED TO MEASURE TIME?

People have always organized their lives by the passing of time. The earliest hunters had to hunt during the hours of daylight. When farming had developed, it was important for farmers to understand the seasons in order to plant their crops at the right time.

Long ago, people realized that the movement of the Sun allowed them to recognize the time of day.

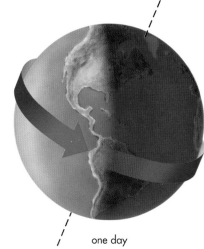

one day

They also realized that the movement of the Moon was regular and could be used to give measurements of roughly one month. Modern life is governed much more by time, and we now depend on highly accurate clocks to measure every second of the day.

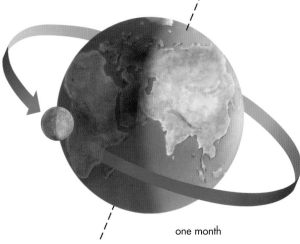

one month

FACT FILE

Modern timepieces are often digital. Such clocks contain electronic circuits which receive digital signals. The clocks receive the signals in binary code which it can understand.

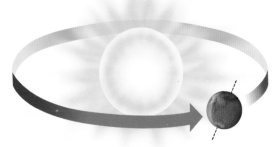

one year

WHY DO BOATS HAVE SAILS?

Nearly three-quarters of the Earth's surface is covered by water, most of it in the seas and oceans. For thousands of years people have been finding ways to cross this water. At first they built rafts, and boats with oars, but around 2900 BC, the Egyptians began to use sails. From then on, sailing ships ruled the seas until a century ago. Today, big ships have engines, but small sailing ships are used for sport, fishing and local trade.

Of course sailing ships are reliant on the wind to power them. Sailors are unable to change the direction of the wind, but they can change the direction of their sailing boats by steering a zigzag course, called tacking.

FACT FILE

Yacht racing is a very popular sport these days. In yacht racing it is very often the efficiency with which a boat tacks, compared with its competitors, that makes it a winner.

WHY DO CARS HAVE ENGINES?

The very first vehicle able to run on the open road was powered by steam. However, it was not until the development of the internal combustion engine in the second half of the nineteenth century that motor transport began to be successful.
Internal combustion engines are usually fuelled by petrol or diesel. This fuel is burnt (or combusted) within metal cylinders. The burning fuel causes a piston to move up and down inside each cylinder. It is this upward and downward movement that is translated into a turning movement by the crankshaft, causing the axles and wheels to turn and the car to move forward. The engine also powers an alternator which generates electrical current. This current is stored in the battery and is used for the car's lights, windscreen wipers, radio and other features such as electric windows.

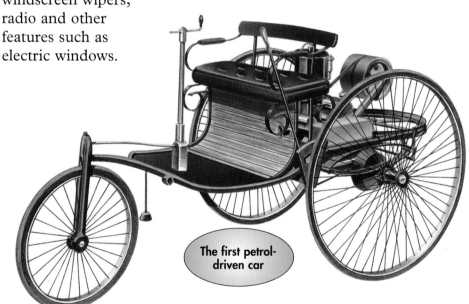

The first petrol-driven car

FACT FILE

Most petrol engines are quite noisy and give off harmful fumes. Quieter and cleaner electric cars are now being designed. However their batteries need continually recharging so they are only used for short distances.

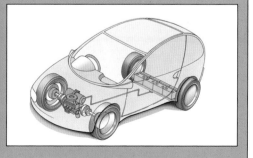

WHY IS FIRE SO HOT?

The answer to this question is really in the fire itself. Fire is a chemical reaction that occurs very quickly and gives off heat and light. The most common is the chemical action between oxygen and a fuel. If heat and light are given off, you have a fire. To make a fire, three things are necessary. The first is a fuel, the second is oxygen and the third thing is heat. Paper or wood that is simply exposed to air does not catch fire. When the fuel becomes hot enough, oxygen can begin to combine freely with it and then it will burst into flames. Every fuel has its own particular temperature at which it begins to burn. This temperature is called the kindling temperature or flash point of the fuel. When something catches fire, it is very important to bring the flames under control as soon as possible. This is especially true when a building catches fire.

FACT FILE

Firefighters need to wear protective clothing that does not conduct heat easily and therefore will not catch fire easily. Fireproof clothing often has a shiny surface, because this helps to reflect the radiated heat away from the body.

WHY CAN WAX BE BOTH NATURAL AND SYNTHETIC?

Wax can be obtained from many fruits, vegetables and plants. Waxes are also produced by animals and are found in minerals and petroleum. There are also synthetic, or man-made waxes. We acquire wax from many different sources.

Carnauba wax is obtained from the leaves of the carnauba palm tree of Brazil. It is a brown wax used in records, floor dressings and candles. Bayberry wax, from the berries of the shrub, is also used for making candles. Worker bees secrete wax that they use in making their honeycombs. This is used in making cosmetics, church candles, polishes, crayons and artificial flowers. Wool wax from wool-bearing animals is called lanolin and it used in some ointments, cosmetics and soaps.

More than 90 per cent of all commercial wax used today is petroleum wax. It has a wide variety of uses because it is odourless, tasteless and chemically inactive.

FACT FILE

Inside a hive, the bees store their honey in a network of wax which is called a honeycomb. Each one is made up of thousands of little six-sided cells. The bees feed on the honey during the cold winter months.

WHY IS ARCHIMEDES REMEMBERED?

Archimedes was a Greek mathematician who lived between about 287 and 212 BC. Archimedes believed in making experiments to prove that his theories worked. He made practical inventions such as the Archimedean screw which is still used today to lift water for irrigation. He also worked out the laws which govern the use of levers and pulleys.

Perhaps the most famous thing he is remembered for is when he jumped out of his bath and ran naked through the streets shouting 'Eureka!' which means 'I've found it!' in English. Whether this story is true or not, he did find that an object displaces its own weight of water when floating or submerged.

FACT FILE

Luigi Galvani (1737–1798) was an Italian scientist. He accidentally noticed that severed frogs' legs twitched when the nerve was touched with a pair of metal scissors during a thunderstorm.

The Archimedian Screw

WHY IS EINSTEIN REMEMBERED?

Albert Einstein (1879–1955) was a physicist who was born in Germany. He developed the theory of relativity, which led to the famous equation $E = mc^2$ (which very few people actually understand). Einstein's work is the basis for most of the modern theories about nature, history and the structure of the Universe. He laid down the rules that govern objects moving close to the speed of light, and explained why travel at this sort of speed could distort time itself. His work also proved invaluable in the development of the atomic bomb. He is remembered as one of the greatest scientists of our time.

FACT FILE

Benjamin Franklin (1706–1790) was an American with many talents. He was a printer, scientist and politician who played an important part in founding the United States. He developed lightning rods to protect buildings from storms.

WHY MUST THE PYRAMID BUILDERS HAVE BEEN GOOD MATHEMATICIANS?

FACT FILE

Mathematical formulae must have been used in the building of pyramids. An example is the Pythagoras Theorem below, a formula for calculating one side of a right-angled triangle, if the other two sides are known.

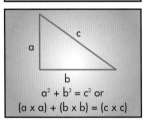

$a^2 + b^2 = c^2$ or
$(a \times a) + (b \times b) = (c \times c)$

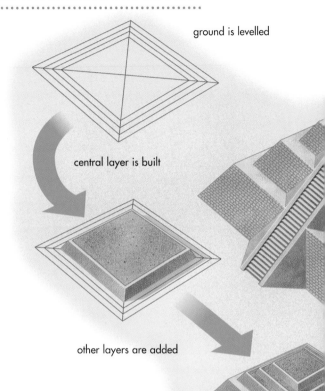

ground is levelled

central layer is built

other layers are added

The Egyptians were building massive pyramids almost 5,000 years ago. We are still not sure how they achieved this without the mechanical lifting and cutting equipment that we have today, but the answer must be that they used huge numbers of slaves to shape and haul the enormous stones with which they were built. Recently, scientists have calculated that as many as 10,000 slaves were probably needed to work on one of these structures.

The shape of a pyramid, which is a three-dimensional figure with flat faces, is called a polyhedron. These huge structures were very carefully designed and constructed. It is clear that the builders must have had a very good knowledge of mathematics to be able to build and measure these vast pyramids with such accuracy.

WHY DO WE NEED NUMBERS?

The building of pyramids

finished pyramid

the layers are built up

Numbers are used to describe the amount of things. We can express numbers in words, by hand gestures or in writing, using symbols or numerals. When we talk about a number we use words (five) rather than the number (5), but when we write we use both words and numerals. Numbers can describe how many objects there are, or their position among lots of objects, for example, 1st or 5th.

Other types of numbers describe how many units of something there are, for example how many kilograms (weight) or metres (length). Numbers are just a convenient way of describing ideas.

FACT FILE				
Roman numerals are still used today for certain purposes. They appear on watch and clock faces and when numbers have a certain importance, such as in the title of a monarch.	I	1	VIII	8
	II	2	IX	9
	III	3	X	10
	IV	4	XX	20
	V	5	L	50
	VI	6	C	100
	VII	7	M	1000

EARTH

AND SPACE

CONTENTS

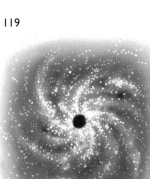

WHY IS THERE NO LIFE ON THE OTHER PLANETS?

As far as we know, there is no form of life on any of the other planets in the Solar System.

Jupiter

It was assumed that light, water and oxygen – as seen at the Earth's surface – were necessary to life and we know that none of the other planets have these surface conditions. However, in the last few years it has been found that some life-forms need neither light nor oxygen as they live in a system which depends on sulphur from deep undersea volcanoes in conditions of extreme heat and pressure. So some scientists hope that life-forms might exist in similar extreme conditions elsewhere in the Solar System. Other possiblities that are being explored (or may be explored in the future) include Saturn's satellite Titan and Jupiter's satellite Europa, as well as several comets to see if they contain the basic materials to support life.

FACT FILE

Mars is a planet that is covered by a stony desert that contains lots of iron oxide. This makes it appear to be a rusty-red colour. The water and oxygen this planet once had are now locked in the rusty iron deposits.

WHY IS GRAVITY ON EARTH NOT THE SAME IN SPACE?

Everything in the Universe exerts a force on everything else. This force is called gravity, or gravitation. The strength of the force of gravity between any two particular objects depends on two things: their individual masses and the distance between them.

The greater an object's mass, the greater its pull on other objects, so the Earth exerts a higher pull on a person than that person does on the Earth.

Earth

The farther two objects are apart, the less the effect of the force of gravity between them: an astronaut floating free 30 metres away from the International Space Station would feel one-ninth of its gravitational pull as an astronaut only 10 metres away.

Astronauts in space experience 'weightlessness' when they are far enough away from the Earth for its gravitational pull to be balanced (or outweighed) by that of the rest of the Universe.

FACT FILE

Although it might seem that gravity carries food and drink down our throats, astronauts are able to eat and drink perfectly well in zero gravity. This is because it is the muscular contractions of the gullet that actually transport food and drink into the stomach.

WHY DO STARS TWINKLE?

Most stars burn steadily and if we could see them from space they would not actually be twinkling at all.

As the light from a star passes through the Earth's atmosphere, it is bent by changes in the air temperature. This makes the light appear to flicker. Because of this effect observatories for studying the stars are situated on mountain-tops. The reason for this is because the higher up you go, the air becomes thinner and it is less likely to cause the twinkling effect.

FACT FILE

Sometimes a giant star explodes and is blown to pieces. This is called a supernova. A supernova explosion sometimes results in a pulsar. A pulsar is a rapidly spinning star that gives off pulses of radio waves.

WHY ARE GALAXIES DIFFERENT SHAPES?

A galaxy is an enormous group of stars which is held together by the force of gravity. Our own galaxy is called the Milky Way and this is in the shape of a spiral. There are possibly as many as 100 billion galaxies in the universe. Many of them are grouped together in clusters with huge areas of space between them and consequently form many irregular shapes.

FACT FILE

The Milky Way is a huge disc-shaped collection of billion of stars and interstellar debris. Most of these stars cannot be seen with the naked eye but their combined light produces a huge milky-looking path across the night sky.

WHY DO WE NEED SPACE STATIONS?

Space stations are usually made up of several modules that are sent into orbit one at a time, and then assembled once in space. Space stations allow the crew to work in space for long periods of time in conditions of zero gravity. While conditions in space capsules and the space shuttle are cramped, space stations are adapted for longer stays in space. Rockets or the space shuttle bring supplies of air and food to the space station and often a replacement crew.

Some space stations, such as the Russian Mir, stayed up for many years and their crews remained in space for months at a time.

FACT FILE

If you blow up a balloon and let it go without tying a knot in the neck, the air will rush out very quickly. When the air goes out one way it pushes the balloon the other way – just like a rocket!

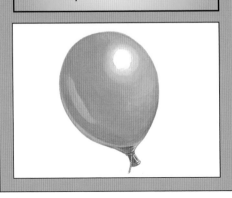

WHY ARE SPACE PROBES IMPORTANT IN SPACE EXPLORATION?

Mir Space Station

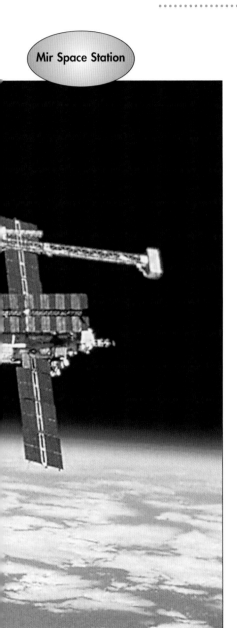

Space probes are small packages of instruments that are launched from the Earth to explore planets. Probes have landed small instrument capsules on Mars and Venus. They take photographs or test the atmosphere of a planet. Some probes use the gravity of other planets to extend their voyages. They pass close by a planet, using its gravity to swing around it and be hurled off towards another planet. Using this very technique the Voyager 2 space probe was able to visit Jupiter, Saturn, Uranus and Neptune. Probes do not have their own rocket power apart from tiny thrusters for steering.

WHY DO ASTRONAUTS NEED TO WEAR SPACESUITS?

A spacesuit is all that stands between an astronaut on a space walk and the emptiness of space. It must supply all his or her needs. There is no breathable atmosphere in space so a spacesuit supplies oxygen to the astronaut.

Within the helmet, headphones and a microphone enable the astronaut to communicate with crew members and mission control. All the joins in the spacesuit must be absolutely airtight. Inside the suit is pressurized like a deep-sea diver's suit. The visor and outer layer of the suit must be tough enough not to be torn or cracked by tiny meteorites that may bounce off the astronaut. A specially treated dark visor protects the astronaut's eyes from the glare of the Sun, while lights can illuminate dark areas.

FACT FILE

As well as supplying air to breathe, space suits have to remove moisture breathed out by the astronaut, so the clear face-place of the suit is not misted up by the cold of space.

WHY DO WE LAUNCH SATELLITES INTO SPACE?

Space satellites have revolutionized communication, making possible everyday developments such as mobile phones and television. Satellites receive signals beamed at them from the Earth and send them on to other places. They are also used in defence communications for checking on the movement of military forces. Satellites can also survey the surface of the Earth, predict weather changes and track hurricanes.

FACT FILE

Navigation satellites enable people on land or at sea to work out their exact map position to within a few metres.

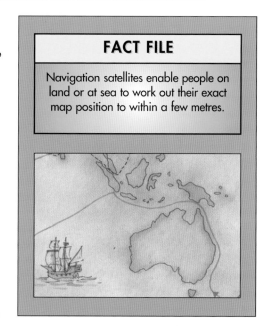

WHY DOES THE MOON SHINE?

The simple answer is that it does not shine; like the Earth, it reflects the light of the Sun. We see light and dark patches, including the 'Man in the Moon' pattern, because different materials on the Moon's surface reflect sunlight differently. The dark areas are lowland areas of ancient lava flows while the brighter patches are even older highland regions.

Because the Moon rotates on its axis in the same amount of time it takes to make one orbit around the Earth we always see the same side of the Moon and did not know what the far side looked like until it was photographed by a Soviet probe, called Lunar 3 (or Lunik 3), in 1959. The far side does not have large lava-filled areas.

Day and night on the Moon are not the same length as on the Earth: each lasts for roughly 14 days. During the day, the temperature may reach as high as 123 °C (253 °F) but can sometimes drop to as low as –233 °C (–387 °F) during the night.

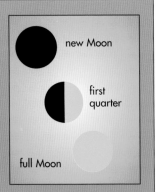

FACT FILE

When the Moon is on the same side of Earth as the Sun, it reflects light away from us. This is new Moon. A week later we see half of the sunlit Moon: this is first quarter. When the Moon is opposite the Sun, we see a full Moon.

new Moon

first quarter

full Moon

WHY DOES THE MOON FOLLOW US WHEN WE DRIVE?

When we are sitting in a car that is moving at speed, objects that are close to the road pass behind us very quickly, but objects that are a few hundred metres away stay in view for a little longer. Objects that are farther away, such as a television mast or a clump of trees at the top of a hill take even longer to go past.

This is because the closer we are to an object, the more quickly the angle we're seeing it at changes as we move along.

The Moon, of course, is much farther away – about 239,000 miles (384,550 kilometres), so the angle between it and us changes much more slowly as we drive along. The reason that it appears to follow us is a trick of the eye and mind: because everything else goes past but the Moon does not, our brains interpret this to mean that it is moving with us.

The Moon

FACT FILE

The ebbing and flowing of tides is caused by the Sun and Moon pulling on the oceans. When the Sun, Earth and Moon are in a line, there are high spring tides.

WHY ARE ASTEROIDS LIKE SMALL PLANETS?

Asteroids are smaller than any of the planets and only a few have a diameter of over 30 kilometres. Asteroids are small rocky or icy bodies that orbit the Sun. They are sometimes called minor planets. Most asteroids are found in an orbit between Mars and Jupiter, and more than 7,000 of them have been identified.

The term asteroid is usually applied to objects that are larger than 1.6 kilometres in diameter. One asteroid, called Ida, has a tiny moon all of its own. This is the smallest known satellite in the Solar System. Asteroids were probably formed at the same time as the planets.

FACT FILE

Many asteroids have struck the Earth already, and many scientists believe that such an impact resulted in the extinction of the dinosaurs about 65 million years ago.

WHY DO METEORS SOMETIMES CRASH INTO THE EARTH?

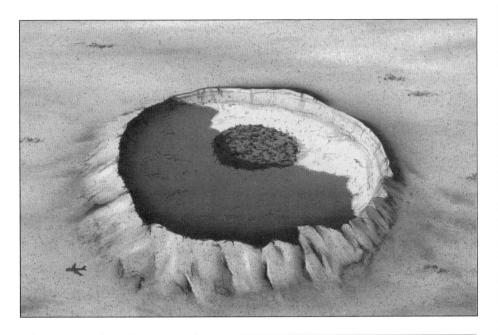

If a lump of rock or metal burns up before it reaches the ground, it is called a meteor or a shooting star. A large meteor that does not burn up as it plunges through the Earth's atmosphere is called a meteorite. It travels so fast it shatters into pieces as it hits the ground. It causes huge shock waves as it lands. The impact crater in the picture above is to be found at Wolf Creek, Australia, and was caused by a huge meteorite or small asteroid. The amount of energy released would be equivalent to hundreds of nuclear weapons.

FACT FILE

The asteroid belt lies between the orbits of Mars and Jupiter. It is thought that this may be the shattered remains of a planet that has been destroyed by Jupiter's enormous gravity.

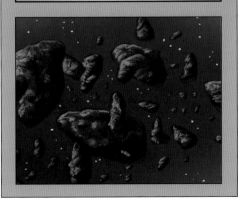

WHY DO NEBULAE EXIST?

Without nebulae stars would not exist in our skies. A nebula is a huge cloud of gas and material that appears to be solid. However, it is mostly composed of dust and gas, slowly condensing into stars.

Stars come into existence in the vast clouds of dust and gas that move through space. A star begins to form when a large number of gas particles whirl together within such a cloud. The whirling particles attract more particles, and as the group of particles slowly gets larger and larger, its gravitational pull gets stronger. The particles form a giant ball of gas.

As the ball grows larger, the particles press down on those below them and pressure builds up inside the ball. Finally the pressure becomes strong enough to raise the temperature of the gases, and the gases begin to glow. When the pressure and temperature inside the ball get very high, nuclear reactions begin to take place and form a star.

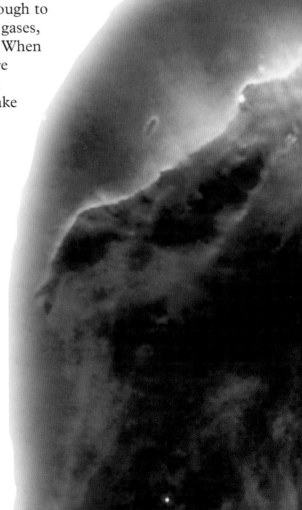

FACT FILE

A black hole is not really a hole but a very tightly-packed object. It is solid and does not reflect any light, so it looks like a hole!

WHY DO STARS DIE?

Stars are huge balls of burning gas that are scattered throughout the Universe. They burn for millions of years, giving off both light and heat. Stars die when they eventually use up all their fuel and burn out. This process may take millions of years.

Towards the end of its life a star starts to run out of hydrogen to power its nuclear fusion. It starts to cool, becoming a red giant. The red giant swells, and the pressure at its centre becomes so great that the star begins to absorb energy instead of emitting it. In a matter of seconds the star collapses, then explodes into a supernova. This is a huge explosion of light and energy that can be seen right across the galaxy.

A Nebula

FACT FILE

In the night sky, all stars appear to be the same size. In fact, they are all different sizes. Some are much bigger than the Sun; others are much smaller than the Earth. The most common stars are the same size as the Sun.

WHY DO WE HAVE NIGHT AND DAY?

As the Earth spins on its axis, the Sun always shines on one side giving us daylight. On the shaded side it is night time. As the Earth continues to turn, the shaded side moves into the Sun's light, and the sunlit side turns away from the light. It takes 24 hours for the Earth to make one complete turn on its axis and our clocks are based on this principle.

In the 1940s people discovered that the Earth speeds up and slows down a little as it spins. We have now developed atomic clocks that can measure time exactly.

FACT FILE

The Earth's axis is an imaginary line through the centre of the Earth. This is what the Earth spins around. You can think of the axis as being a stick pushed through the middle of an orange.

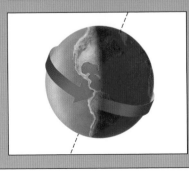

WHY DO WE HAVE SEASONS?

We have seasons because the Earth is tilted on its axis. As the Earth moves round the Sun, the hemisphere tilted towards the Sun receives more sunlight, and this is summer time. The days are longer and the weather is warmer because of the extra amount of sunlight. The hemisphere tilted away from the Sun receives less sunshine, has shorter days and is cooler. This is winter time. The area near to the Equator is always exposed to the Sun's rays, so it is warm all the year round. This means that there is little difference between the seasons.

FACT FILE

Coloured sunsets happen when light is scattered by dust and water particles in the air, as the Sun sets. The farther the light has to pass through the air, the more likely it is to be scattered causing the red colouration.

123

WHY IS THE SKY BLUE?

As the Sun's light passes through the atmosphere, its rays are scattered by tiny particles of pollen, soot and dust to be found there. As blue light is scattered most, the sky appears blue. At sunset and sunrise, sunlight has further to travel to reach us. Only red light can be seen because the blue light has been absorbed by the atmosphere.

FACT FILE

The amount of rain which falls is known as precipitation. This diagram shows the average annual precipitation level of the continents of the world

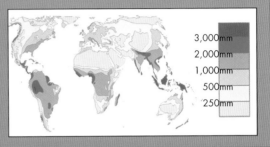

3,000mm
2,000mm
1,000mm
500mm
250mm

WHY DON'T ALL CLOUDS PRODUCE RAIN?

When a potential rain cloud forms, warm moist air rises from the ground or from the sea below until it becomes cool enough for the water vapour in it to condense into water droplets.

As more vapour condenses, the cloud gets thicker and the droplets continue to grow and start to collide with each other to form larger drops of water as they move upwards in the rising air.

Eventually, when they become large enough, the effect of gravity will overcome the strength of the rising air and they will start to fall, merging with other drops and growing further as they do so.

When they get to the bottom of the cloud, if the air below is cold, they will fall as rain. If, however, the air beneath the cloud is warm, they will simply evaporate and the water vapour will start the whole process again. High up in clouds, this process also occurs, but with ice crystals that build up layer upon layer of ice and may eventually fall as hail.

FACT FILE

Rainbows occur in the sky when drops of rain in the air act as prisms to split the light into the seven colours of the spectrum. This usually happens just after a fall of rain.

WHY DO VOLCANOES ERUPT?

At about two miles below the surface of the Earth the temperature is high enough to boil water. If it were possible to dig down 30 miles, the temperature would be about 2,200 degrees fahrenheit. This is hot enough even to melt rocks. At the centre of the Earth scientists believe that the temperature could be as high as 10,000 degrees fahrenheit.

When rock melts, it expands and needs more space. When the pressure is greater than the roof of rock above it, it bursts out causing an eruption. When the volcano erupts it throws out hot, gaseous liquid called lava or solid particles that look like cinders and ash. The material piles up around the opening and a cone-shaped mound is formed.

FACT FILE

A *dormant* volcano is one that is actually 'sleeping'. A dormant volcano might erupt in the future. An *extinct* volcano, on the other hand, will not become active again.

WHY ARE VOLCANIC BOMBS DANGEROUS?

A major volcanic eruption can send boulders flying high into the air. These boulders, called volcanic bombs, can be very large. Most of the material thrown of the erupting volcano is ash, which forms a huge cloud. Steam and sulphurous gases are also released and these can be extremely dangerous to bystanders.

On August 24, in the year AD 79, Mount Vesuvius, a volcano in Italy, violently erupted. The lava, stones, and ashes thrown up by the volcano completely buried two nearby towns.

FACT FILE

Krakatau, Indonesia was a volcanic island which had been dormant for over two centuries. In 1883, a huge volcanic eruption occurred, destroying two-thirds of the island.

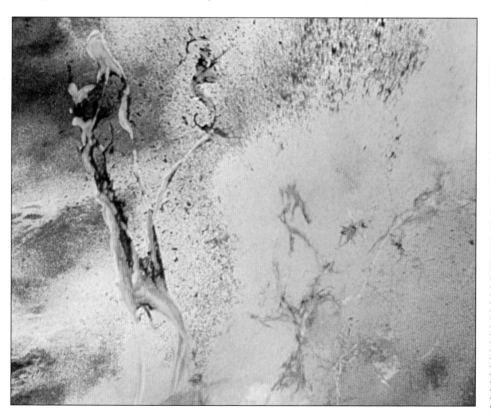

WHY IS THE PACIFIC PLATE ALWAYS MOVING?

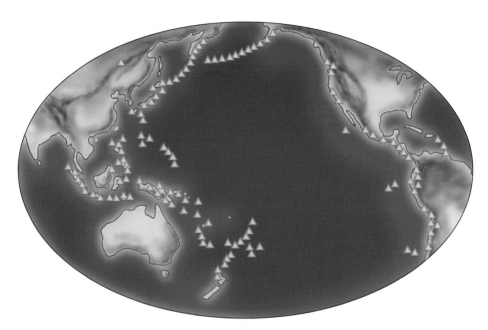

The Earth's crust is not one unbroken piece. It is made up of many pieces that fit together like a giant jigsaw puzzle. These pieces, called plates, ride on soft, partly melted rock moving underneath them. The pieces push against each other with spectacular effects. Earthquakes split the Earth's crust, volcanoes are formed, new land is made, and huge mountain ranges are pushed skywards.

The plates are never still, they are always moving. In one year alone they can move about 2.5 centimetres, about as much as your fingernails grow in the same amount of time.

FACT FILE

When water seeps into the ground and reaches hot rock, it boils violently. This produces steam which can shoot the water out of cracks, causing a geyser. Geysers can be very spectacular and some shoot water as high as 500 metres into the air.

WHY IS GERARDUS MERCATOR REMEMBERED?

TELL ME WHY : EARTH AND SPACE

FACT FILE

A map must be as easy to read as possible, which means that symbols and colours can often give more information than words. A key explains what the symbols and colours mean.

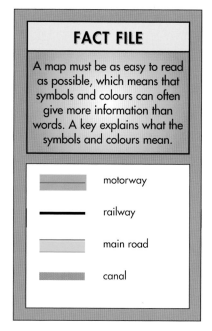

motorway

railway

main road

canal

Gerhard Kremer (1512–94) was called Gerardus Mercator, meaning merchant, because he made maps for merchants travelling from country to country. In 1569 he made a world map using a projection that has come to be known as Mercator's projection.

It is not possible to draw the curved surface of the globe accurately on a flat sheet of paper. He showed how to convert the rounded shape of the world into a cylindrical shape, which could be unrolled to make a flat map. However, this can distort the size of countries in the far north and south. But by dividing the Earth into 'orange peel' segments it gave a truer image of the size of the countries.

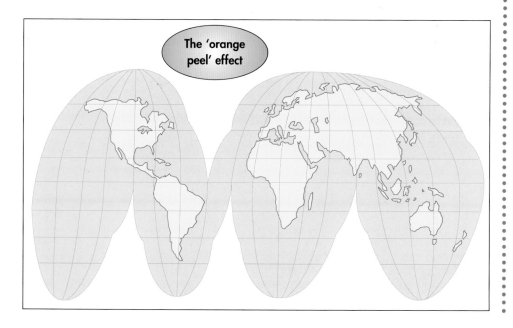

The 'orange peel' effect

WHY IS THE OCEAN SALTY?

The answer is that no one really knows. Salt (also known as Sodium Chloride), like many other substances, is dissolved from rocks on the land and drains into the oceans, from which water evaporates leaving the salt behind, but why there is so much of it is unclear.

The salt in the Earth's oceans is vital in maintaining the currents – like the Gulf Stream – that circulate heat throughout the oceans and regulate the planet's temperature. In one of these currents, warm, salty surface water flows north from the Caribbean, until it reaches cool fresh water from melting glaciers on Greenland and north-eastern Canada. There it sinks to the ocean floor and flows back towards the equator, where it will rise and start the process again. One of the ideas that worries some environmental scientists is that if the Greeland or Canadian ice melts too quickly because of Global Warming, this circulation pattern will stop, and places like New York and London could become much cooler.

FACT FILE

The Earth has five oceans. These are the Pacific, Atlantic, Indian, Arctic and Antarctic. In addition, there are several substantial seas such as the Mediterranean and the Black Sea.

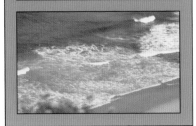

WHY WERE THE FIRST EXPLORERS SO PIONEERING?

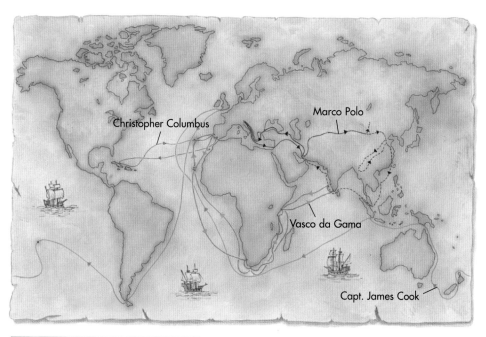

FACT FILE

In 1492 Christopher Columbus set out to find a new route to India and the Far East, in order to open up trading links for Spain. He arrived at the Bahamas, off the American coast, where he mistakenly called the native people 'Indians'.

About 50,000 years ago, the first explorers sailed from Southeast Asia to colonize Australia and New Guinea, which were joined together at that time. Later on, people crossed from Siberia into Alaska, passing over a land bridge that has since disappeared.

Marco Polo began his voyage to China in 1271. He reached his destination but parts of his journey (shown above with a dotted line) are in doubt. Christopher Columbus discovered Cuba and Haiti in 1492. In 1497 Vasco da Gama set out to find a sea route to India by sailing around the southern tip of Africa. Captain James Cook made three voyages to the South Seas. During his first voyage he discovered Australia.

WHY DOES FOG FORM OVER WATER?

Warm air holds more moisture than cold air, so when it chills to a certain point – the dew- or saturation point – water will condense into droplets of fog, cloud or dew, depending on circumstances. At sea, fog forms when warm air currents travel over colder water and the air is chilled until it reaches dewpoint and condenses. This is the fog that often occurs around coasts.

Over land, when warm moist air just above land chills rapidly on clear, calm, nights, mist or fog will form. Technically, mist is when visibility is reduced to more than 1,000 metres, fog when it is less than 1,000 metres and thick fog when it is less than 100 metres.

FACT FILE

Over land, mist and fog commonly form in enclosed valleys, where cooling air flows gently down the sides of the hills to sit on the bottom of the valley floor where the water vapour condenses.

WHY IS SNOW WHITE?

Given that water is clear, why does snow appear white? It is to do with its complex crystal structure. Every snow flake, whether large or small, is basically hexagonal in structure with complicated facets that reflect and scatter the light in all directions so that the colours mix to re-form white light.

In glaciers, the red and yellow parts of visible light are more readily absorbed by the hard-packed ice than violet and blue, so many glaciers look blue, rather than white, both from above and from tourist tunnels burrowed through them.

FACT FILE

The Inuit people live in the icy lands of the Arctic North. They are self-sufficient and live a life on the move, hunting and fishing to survive. They build homes, called igloos, out of solid snow.

WHY DO WE STILL HAVE GLACIERS TODAY?

At the height of the Ice Age, actually the most recent in a series, ice sheets reached as far south as the current site of the River Thames and Scotland was covered in thousands of feet of ice. Although the last ice sheet melted from Britain about 12,000 years ago, high in the Alps, Pyrenees and other mountains, glaciers remain as remnants of that period, although many are currently shrinking rapidly. Some scientists think that the Earth is currently undergoing an 'Interglacial' – a period of warming during a longer Ice Age – and that the ice may, at some point in future, begin to thicken and advance again.

FACT FILE

Glaciers typically gouge out U-shaped, flat-bottomed valleys as they grind their way down between mountains carrying boulders that weigh thousands of tons with them. The circular area where the glacier first forms at the head of a valley is called a glacial cirque.

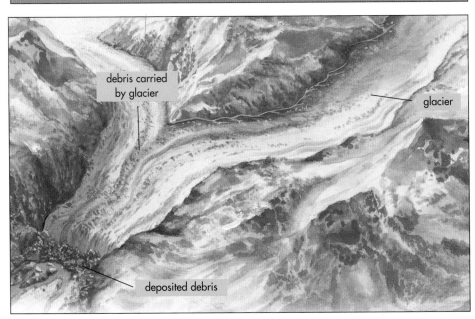

debris carried by glacier

glacier

deposited debris

WHY DO WATERFALLS EXIST?

Waterfalls occur where the course of a stream or river has to make a drop from one level to another.

Many waterfalls are created when water flows from a hard rock to a softer one that is eroded more easily. Over thousands – even millions – of years, the softer rock is continually worn away forming a steep-sided drop into a deep pool. Niagara Falls on the border of Canada and the United States is one example of this kind of waterfall.

Other waterfalls occur where glaciers have ground out rock and after their retreat meltwater from higher up the mountain drops to the valley floor below.

FACT FILE

Angel Falls in Venezuela, South America is the highest waterfall in the world , though both Niagara Falls and Victoria Falls have a greater volume of water.

WHY ARE RAINFORESTS IN DANGER?

Rainforests are tropical evergreen forests. The climate is warm and moist all year round and offers an extraordinarily wide range of habitats for living things.

Rainforests are being cut down at an alarming rate for two main reasons. Both large commercial farming companies and individual families clear the forest to gain land to cultivate and graze animals. The rainforest soil, though, is not really suitable for agriculture.

Another reason the forests have been felled is to supply tropical hardwoods for furniture-making and buildings. Woods such as mahogany have been highly prized in wealthy countries for hundreds of years.

FACT FILE

Many areas of tropical rainforest are burned. The result after one or two years is useless, infertile land that is prone to flash floods. Rainwater strips away the topsoil, dumping it into rivers.

WHY IS TOO MUCH WATER BAD FOR FARM LAND?

Erosion is one of the most powerful ways in which the Earth's surface is being altered. Moving ice and flowing water wear away the surface and cut out valleys. Along the coast, tides and wave action wears away exposed cliffs, and currents carry away sand mud to be deposited elsewhere. Floodwater rapidly washes away fertile soil which can cause the loss of much fertile land. The bare ground becomes eroded because there is little vegetation to slow the run-off of rainwater.

FACT FILE

Low-level land becomes flooded very easily. It often takes months for the land to recover from flooding.

WHY IS MACHINERY IMPORTANT ON LARGE FARMS?

Machinery has made it possible for the work of a dozen farm workers to be done twice as quickly as by one worker. There are fewer people working on the land in developed countries than ever before.

Machinery also has a large effect on the environment as well, as hedges and ditches are removed to allow larger machines to work the enormous fields. Crops have also been bred for the machine age too. They need to ripen together, not over a period of time, so that machinery can harvest them in one operation.

There are still many parts of the world where traditional farming methods are used, but the use of machinery is increasing year by year.

FACT FILE

Arable farming is the growing and harvesting of crops, particularly where the ground is ploughed between harvests. Arable farming is of enormous importance to the world's population, since most of us rely on grains or vegetables for our staple foods.

WHY DOES TERRACING HELP FARMERS?

The terracing system of farming is particularly important where people have to grow their food on steep, erosion prone slopes. This agricultural system has been in use for three thousand years in hillside regions of Mexico.

Terracing slows the rate of intense rainfall runoff which often comes in bursts, thereby minimizing erosion while still conserving water. After rainfall the terraces enabled captured water to slowly percolate into the fields, making for an efficient irrigation system.

ANCIENT

HISTORY

CONTENTS

WHY DID THE FIRST HUMANS LOOK MORE LIKE APES?

Scientists believe that humans and apes had a common ancestor. About 10 million years ago, some apes left the trees to walk on the open plains. They had large brains, and used their fingers to pick up food. About 4 million years ago, the human-like ape *Australopithecus* (southern ape) lived in Africa. It probably used sticks or stones as tools, in the same way that chimpanzees do. It walked upright, had long limbs, and its body was covered with hair. The first human species was *Homo habilis* (handy man), who lived in East Africa 2 million years ago. By 1.5 million years ago, the more advanced *Homo erectus* (upright man) had appeared, and by 500,000 years ago Homo erectus had learned to make fire. They communicated in some form of language, and worked together gathering plants and hunting animals for food.

◄ Modern man

Neanderthal man ►

Upright man

FACT FILE

Neanderthals were the first humans to bury their dead. Archaeologists have found evidence of Neanderthal burial ceremonies. The remains of tools and meat have been found in the graves, showing that the dead were buried with care.

WHY WAS THE STONE AGE SO-CALLED?

The Stone Age was named because stone was the most important material used by the first tool-makers. These early stone-crafting techniques show surprising skill. Axes and scrapers were made from flint. Spear heads were shaped from deer antlers. The hand axe was probably the most important early Stone Age tool.

Handy man

Southern ape

Stone Age people hunted with bows, spears and flint axes. On the American grasslands, groups of hunters drove to extinction large grazing animals such as mastodons and giant bison. The humans' intelligence, weapons and teamwork made up for their comparative lack of strength and speed.

FACT FILE

People discovered how to make fire by using a simple wooden stick called a fire drill. The drill was turned quickly over a piece of dry wood until it produced enough heat to start the fire.

Hand axe

Scraper

Spear head

WHY DID THE ABORIGINES BELIEVE IN 'DREAM TIME'?

The Aborigines probably reached Australia overland. They lived by gathering food and hunting. Along the coast they fished with nets, basket traps and spears. In the bush they used fire to drive animals into traps and made poisons from leaves and roots to drug fish in pools. They wore no clothes and rubbed animal fats onto their bodies to protect themselves from the cold.

Aboriginal rock artists looked 'beneath the skin' to show a person's bones or organs. Paintings of people and animals are found at sites linked in Aboriginal belief to the Dream Time. This is the time when the spirits were supposed to have created the world.

FACT FILE

The Aborigines used ritual boomerangs in magical dances, decorated with secret symbols. They were also used for hunting purposes and for war.

WHY DID CAVE PAINTERS PAINT?

Many thousands of years ago people painted pictures of bulls, horses and antelopes on the walls of their caves. We will never be sure why they actually did this – perhaps it was to make magic and bring people luck in their hunting. Another theory was that it may have been part of their religion.

Cave artists used natural paints which were made from coloured earth and plant extracts. These paints have often been hidden from view for thousands of years. Viewed by the flickering light of burning torches, as they would have been when first painted, the animals almost seem to come to life.

FACT FILE

Woolly mammoths were found painted on the walls of caves. As well as being an important source of meat, woolly mammoths provided skins for clothing and shelter. Their tusks were also carved into tools and ornaments.

WHY WERE THE PEOPLE OF MESOPOTAMIA CALLED SUMERIANS?

About 7,000 years ago, farmers began to move into an area of land between the Tigris and the Euphrates rivers. This fertile land was called Mesopotamia, in what is now called Iraq. In the south of Mesopotamia was the land known as Sumer. The Sumerians, as they became known, were a very inventive race. They developed the first form of writing and recording numbers.

The Sumerians drew pictures on soft clay with a pointed reed. The pictures were drawn downwards in lines, from the right-hand side. Later, they started to write across the tablet from left to right. The reed tip became wedge shaped, as did the marks it made.

FACT FILE

Reed houses were built using reeds cut down from the marshes around the Tigris and Euphrates rivers. The Sumerians also made canoes from these reeds.

WHY IS THE INVENTION OF THE WHEEL CREDITED TO MESOPOTAMIA?

FACT FILE

The wheel was first used by the Sumerians in making pottery in about 3500 BC. Around 300 years later this invention was adapted for a startling new use – that of transportation.

The Sumerians were also credited for the revolutionary invention of the wheel and the plough. They grew bumper crops of cereals, which they traded for items they needed: wood, building stone or metals. Wheeled carts and their skills in writing helped them develop long-distance trade.

The first wheels were made of planks of solid wood held together with crosspieces. They were clumsy and heavy at the beginning. In time, lighter wheels were made; these had many spokes. The first ploughs were also made of wood with the blade made from bronze.

WHY WERE ATHENS AND SPARTA RIVAL STATES?

The Greeks defeating the Persians at the battle of Salamis

Athens was a rich and cultured state. Among its citizens were astronomers, mathematicians, thinkers, writers and artists. Although this was a society with slaves, the rulers had vision, and its government was the first real democracy.

Athens had the best navy in Greece while Sparta had the best army. Sparta's economy, like that of Athens, was based on slave workers but there was no democracy. Sport was encouraged, and girls as well as boys were expected to be fit and athletic. Sparta was run like an army camp, in which everyone was expected to obey. Boys as young as seven were taken from home and trained to be soldiers.

FACT FILE

Broken pieces of pottery were used for letter-writing in the Greek world. Clay fragments are still found today, with business notes written on them.

WHY WAS TRADE IMPORTANT TO THE GREEKS?

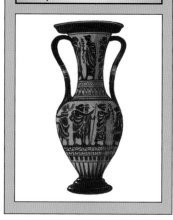

Towns in Greece were a centre for government, religion and trade. In the marketplace farmers sold produce such as cheese, wheat, meat, eggs, sheepskins and olive oil. Fast-food sellers did a brisk lunchtime trade in sausages and pancakes. In the dusty lanes around the marketplace, skilled craftworkers carried on their businesses. They included sandal-makers, potters, tanners (who prepared animal skins), armourers, blacksmiths and jewellers. Wherever they settled, Greek farmers relied on three main crops: grapes, olives and grain. Most colonies were near the sea and fishermen sold freshly caught fish in the markets.

A Greek country house

WHY IS THE HISTORY OF AGAMEMNON'S MASK UNCLEAR?

The Myceneans were warlike people who lived in Greece, possibly from around 1900 BC. By 1600 BC they were trading in the Aegean, and after the fall of Crete they became the major power in the region. The Mycenean rulers lived in hilltop citadels overlooking cities protected by thick stone walls.

The mask of Agamemnon

The city of Mycenae was at the heart of their civilization. People entered Mycenae through the Lion Gate, a great stone gateway from which a path led straight to the royal palace. Graves of the ruling family, filled with treasure and personal possessions for the afterlife were found near the gate in AD 1876.

Weakened by interstate warfare, the Mycenean cities were destroyed and lost. During an excavation of the graves at Mycenae in the late 1800s, the so-called 'mask of Agamemnon' was uncovered. It is unclear of the origin of this mask because so much of the cities and their history were destroyed, but it is believed to be the mask of an earlier king.

FACT FILE

The Myceans had forms of writing which they used in business and government. They wrote on clay tablets and possibly also in ink on papyrus, like the Egyptians.

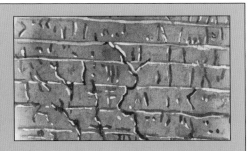

WHY WERE GODS SO IMPORTANT TO THE ANCIENT GREEKS?

The ancient Greeks believed in many different gods. The most important of these were a family of supernatural beings who lived on Mount Olympus and watched over humanity. Certain gods looked after the harvest; others cared for wild animals, the sea, war and so on. The Romans took over many of these Greek gods and gave them Latin names.

They believed the gods could and did interfere in human affairs, bringing success or disaster. King of the gods was Zeus, whom the Romans called Jupiter.

The Minoans, from the island of Crete in the Mediterranean Sea, favoured goddesses in their worship, including the snake goddess who protected the home.

The snake goddess

FACT FILE

According to legend, King Minos kept a half-human, half-bull called the Minotaur in his palace at Knossos.

WHY WAS THE MEGALITHIC ERA SO-CALLED?

More than 5,000 years ago Europeans were building spectacular stone monuments. Many of these are still standing today, as mysterious relics of a long-gone society.

These enormous stones are called megaliths (which literally means 'big stones'). Some were set up on their own, others in groups or in circles. Some megaliths marked the burial place of an important ruler, while others seem to have had a religious meaning.

Tall single stones (menhirs), stone slab-tombs (dolmens) and the remains of large circles of stones and wooden posts (henges) are still standing today.

Stonehenge is an example of remainders from the Megalithic era.

Stonehenge

FACT FILE

Rock tombs, slab tombs (such as this dolmen) and stone circles and temples lie scattered across Europe. Many have been discovered on the island of Malta.

WHY WAS STONEHENGE BUILT?

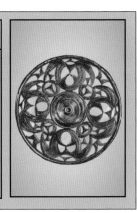

When we try to learn of the accomplishments of ancient man, we usually have to search or dig for evidence. But there is a case where all the evidence has been left standing in a huge structure, and we still cannot figure out what it is, what it was used for, and exactly who built it! This is Stonehenge. It is a complicated structure on the outside of which is a circular ditch, with an entrance gap.

Stonehenge was built in stages between 1800 and 1400 BC. During the second stage of building, blue stones from the Preseli mountains in Wales were hauled onto the site in an astonishing feat of organization and transport.

Local stones were added in the third stage and were up to 10 metres long and weighed 50 tonnes.

The Stonehenge builders had only stone or bronze tools to work with. They had no machines and yet they tackled huge digging works. They buried their chieftains, with treasures and food for the next world, beneath mounds of earth they called barrows.

WHY IS BOADICEA REMEMBERED?

Boadicea (Boudicca) was the queen of the Iceni, a tribe of Celts living in eastern England. Her husband was a governor, who worked with the Romans. After his death the Romans tried to take control. Boadicea led a rebellion, which sacked the towns of Colchester and London, until the Roman armies marched against her. The Romans defeated the Iceni and their Celtic allies. She is renowned for fighting from a chariot, and the Romans had to develop special tactics to combat these fast-moving warriors. Boadicea ended her own life by taking poison to avoid being captured.

FACT FILE

Celtic poetry - 'STORM AT SEA'
Tempest on the plain of Lir
Bursts its barriers far and near
And upon the rising tide
Wind and noisy winter ride
Winter throws a shining spear.

Queen Boadicea on her chariot

WHY DO WE KNOW SO LITTLE ABOUT CELTIC CULTURE?

The Celts came from central Europe, although their previous origins are unclear. Around 500 BC, perhaps to escape wars with their Germanic neighbours, they began to move westwards. Groups of people settled in what are now Spain, France, Britain and Ireland. Celts were warlike and their arrival usually led to fighting.

The Celts were artistic people. They loved stories and music, and they made beautiful jewellery and metalwork decorated with abstract designs and animal shapes.

They had no written language, passing on their legends of gods and heroes in stories around the fire. Most of what we know of the Celts today comes from the writings of their enemies, such as the Romans. The Celts themselves left a legacy of art and legend, and language: Welsh, Breton, Cornish, Irish and Scottish Gaelic are all Celtic languages.

FACT FILE

The Celts often constructed their settlements on hilltops which could be easily defended. They are identified by circular defensive ditches that still survive in former Celtic areas.

An example of Celtic art

WHY IS CONFUCIUS REMEMBERED?

Confucius

Confucius was an ancient Chinese philosopher who taught the need for moral responsibility and virtue. His teachings did not make much impact during his lifetime, but they later became the central part of Chinese moral and religious thinking.

Confucius probably lived from 551 to 479 BC, in the time of the Zhou dynasty. The Zhou was the longest-lasting group of Chinese rulers, who governed the country from 1122 to 256 BC. Confucianism was probably the most important feature in Chinese life until the appearance of Communism in the 20th century. Confucianism resembles a religion, but instead of worshipping gods it is a guide to morality and good government.

Although Confucius lived thousands of years ago, his influence in everyday life is still strong in China today.

FACT FILE

The oldest printed book known is the Diamond Sutta, a Buddhist scroll made from sheets of paper printed with woodblocks. It was made in China in AD 868.

WHY ARE THE TERRACOTTA WARRIORS FAMOUS?

In China the powerful Qin dynasty came to power in the 3rd century BC. They swiftly conquered their neighbours to make a large empire covering most of modern China. The Qin emperor Shi Huangdi standardized weights and measures and introduced a single form of currency. He is best remembered for his construction of the Great Wall of China which stretches for 2,250 km across the north of China.

When the emperor died a huge tomb was built to hold his body. It was filled with a guardian army of thousands of life-sized terracotta (or pottery) warriors. Each figure was individually modelled. The figures were placed in three pits inside the large complex surrounding the emperor's tomb.

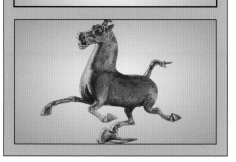

WHY IS THE SPHINX SUCH A MYSTERY?

Religion played an important part in Egyptian life. The Egyptians believed in many gods and goddesses. Gods looked after every aspect of life. Every town and city had its own god, too. Temples were dedicated to a particular god or a dead pharaoh. Pyramids are the oldest stone structures in the world. They were built as tombs, to keep the body of the dead king safe for eternity and perhaps to ease his passage to the heavens. The Great Sphinx is a mysterious rock sculpture with a human head on the body of a lion. This was built near the pyramids, outside modern Cairo, but the exact reason is unknown. Historians believe it is older than the pyramids themselves.

FACT FILE

The sun god Ra was often portrayed simply as a sun disk. He appeared in other forms too, including a cat, a bird and a lion.

The Great Sphinx

WHY DID THE EGYPTIANS MAKE MUMMIES?

Tutankhamun

The Egyptians believed in an afterlife to which human souls journeyed after death. They thought it important that the bodies of the dead should be preserved for life in the next world, and so they developed techniques for making 'mummies'.

The dead person's organs were removed and the body was embalmed and dried, using salts and chemicals, and then wrapped in linen bandages. It was then placed inside a coffin. Even animals such as cats and monkeys were sometimes mummified. Many thousands of mummies must have been made, but only about 1,000 survive today.

Tutankhamun (pictured above) became king of Egypt at the age of nine and died when he was about 18. His tomb is one of more than 60 royal tombs around the Valley of the Kings. Its four rooms contained more than 5,000 objects which included ostrich feathers, model ships, a throne and a gold death mask.

WHY DOES JERICHO HAVE A PLACE IN JEWISH HISTORY?

The Bible records that Abraham had two sons, Ishmael (the ancestor of the Arabs) and Isaac. Isaac had two sons, Esau and Jacob, and Jacob (also called Israel) had 12 sons. These sons became the heads of the Twelve Tribes, the Israelites of the Bible.

The Israelites became wealthy and powerful people. Perhaps they are remembered best for their conquering of the city of Jericho. At God's command the walls of Jericho tumbled down at the sound of the Israelite army shouting and banging their drums.

FACT FILE

Solomon was the son of David, an Israelite king who ruled from 1010 to 970 BC. David defeated the Philistines and enlarged the kingdom, making Jerusalem its capital city. Soloman was responsible for building the sacred Temple in Jerusalem.

WHY IS THE DOME OF THE ROCK CELEBRATED BY TWO RELIGIONS?

The Dome of the Rock which stands in Jerusalem is worshipped by both the Jews and also the Muslims as a holy shrine.

Firstly the Jews believe that the Dome of the Rock is built over the rock on which Abraham, on God's orders, prepared to sacrifice his son to Isaac.

Secondly, the Muslims believe that Muhammad rose to heaven from the very same rock.

FACT FILE

Moses, the leader of the Hebrew people, receives the two tablets from God. The stone tablets bear the Ten Commandments, as described in the Old Testament. They became the basis for Jewish law.

WHY DID THE ASSYRIAN EMPIRE BECOME THE PERSIAN EMPIRE?

Persia grew from the rubble of the defeated Assyrian empire. In 612 BC Nineveh, the Assyrian capital, fell. This left Babylon and Media to wrestle over the remains of the empire. In 550 BC the Persian king Cyrus defeated the Medes and made himself ruler of a new empire. It was known as the Achaemenid Empire. The Persians were good fighters with cavalry and iron weapons, and their military energy proved too strong for their neighbours.

FACT FILE

Ten thousand soldiers called the Immortals formed the core of the Persian army. Each spearman or archer was instantly replaced if killed or became sick.

The ruins of Persepolis (below), the capital of the Persian Empire, lie near the modern city of Shiraz, in southwest Iran. Part of the ruined palace of Darius I is still standing.

Darius I

WHY WAS PERSIA A WELL-ORGANIZED EMPIRE?

Darius I ruled Persia from 521 to 486 BC. He was a very able administrator. He organized the empire into provinces, each governed by a satrap. A satrap was like a king, but not as powerful as the emperor himself whose word was final. He encouraged trade through the use of coins and new canals. Darius and his son, Xerxes, tried to bring Greece within their empire, but failed. However Persia stayed rich and powerful until 331 BC, when it was conquered by Alexander the Great.

FACT FILE

The Persian Empire stretched from North Africa as far as the Caucasus Mountains in the north, and the borders of India in the east.

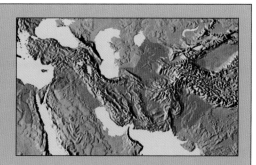

WHY WAS THE ROMAN ARMY SO SUCCESSFUL?

The 'tortoise' formation

The Roman army invented a method of warfare that persisted for 2,000 years. Its troops were rigorously trained and exercised and divided into small detachments under the control of officers. Roman soldiers wore effective armour, and developed tactics that allowed them to fight successfully against almost any enemy. They were particularly good at defence. They used to close ranks and protect themselves with large shields, which deflected arrows and spears, until they reached close quarters and could use their own weapons. The group of soldiers shown above was called the 'tortoise' formation and it proved to be impregnable against their Celtic foes.

FACT FILE

Emperor Trajan built a monument 30 metres high to the Roman army. This section shows Roman legionaires, who were builders as well as fighters, constructing a fort.

WHY DID THE ROMANS BREAK DOWN MOST OF THEIR EMPIRE?

FACT FILE

Hadrian's Wall was built across from the east to the west coasts in an attempt to keep the northern tribes out of the occupied areas.

It soon became evident that the Roman Empire was far too big to survive in its original form. A huge civil service and army were needed to maintain the empire, and these became extremely expensive. Also there were numerous rebellions in different parts of the empire, mostly headed by army commanders with designs on becoming emperor. Eventually, in AD 284, Emperor Diocletian broke the Roman Empire into smaller self-governing units, each with its own army. The whole empire was split into two sections: Eastern and Western. Eventually the Roman Empire was weakened to such an extent that it was successfully attacked and overrun by invading barbarians.

Part of Hadrian's Wall

The Sermon on the Mount

WHY DID THE ROMANS PERSECUTE CHRISTIANS?

The teachings of Jesus were spread widely by His followers after His death. At first, the Christians were ignored by the Romans, especially as they did not join in the Jewish rebellion against Roman rule in AD 66. However, the early Christians began to travel around the Roman Empire, and when they reached Rome they began to recruit new followers. The Roman authorities became concerned that this new religion would threaten the established order.

The Romans did not object to the new religion itself, but they did object to the fact that it denied the emperor's divinity. The new religion appealed to the poor and to the slaves, and its popularity was seen as a threat to Roman society.

FACT FILE

The symbol of a fish was used by the early Christians in Rome as a secret symbol to identify themselves to other Christians. The symbol was simple and quick to draw. It was not likely to be noticed by the Romans.

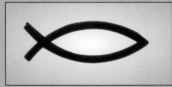

WHY WERE THE DEAD SEA SCROLLS HIDDEN?

The Dead Sea Scrolls are religious writings that were first discovered in 1947, hidden in caves near the Dead Sea. The dry atmosphere of the caves had the effect of preserving the scrolls. About 800 scrolls have been found, mostly in a place called Qumbran in Israel. They date from between 150 BC and AD 68, and they include all of the books of the Old Testament, or Hebrew Bible, except for Esther.

Scholars believe that the scrolls were concealed by members of a religious sect called the Essenes, who lived in the isolated community. They hid the scrolls to keep them safe during political unrest in the area, where they remained hidden for hundreds of years.

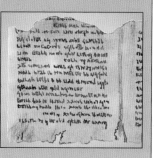

The museum in Jerusalem which holds the Dead Sea Scrolls

WHY WAS ATTILA THE HUN SO FEARED?

Attila the Hun

Attila was the ruler of the Hun kingdom, in what is now called Hungary. The Huns began to expand beyond this area, conquering surrounding countries until they controlled a region from the Rhine to the Caspian Sea, extending all the way to the Baltic. The Huns were among the fiercest of the many barbarian tribes who eventually destroyed the power of the Roman Empire. Attila, who is still renowned for his cruelty and the ferocity of his troops, led the Huns from their homeland and almost conquered Europe. He forced the Eastern Roman Empire to pay him a fee in exchange for not attacking them. He also demanded to marry the sister of the emperor of the Western Empire, with half the empire as a dowry, a request which was refused and caused bloodshed.

FACT FILE

A Roman coin stamped with the head of the Emperor Hadrian. During his reign, he personally visited nearly every province in the Roman Empire.

WHY DO ISLAMIC BELIEVERS FOLLOW THE KORAN?

The Koran is the holy book of the Islamic religion. It contains the words of Allah as revealed to Mohammed by the archangel Gabriel in a series of visions. The Koran is a series of verses describing the ways in which Muslims should conduct their lives. It specifies daily prayers, and emphasizes the need for brotherly love and charity between Muslims. Although Muslims do not worship Mohammed, they show him the greatest respect. They believe that the Koran is the word of Allah and was not composed by Mohammed.

The Holy Koran

WHY WAS FUJIWARA JAPAN A STRONG EMPIRE?

Prince Shotoku ruled Japan from AD 593 to 622, strongly encouraged by Chinese ways. Shotoku believed that the Japanese emperor should be all-powerful, like the ruler of China. In AD 858, however, the emperor lost control to a strong noble family called the Fujiwaras. The Fujiwaras had built up their power in the countryside, where they owned huge estates. Other nobles too had built up small 'empires' of their own.

The Fujiwaras gradually won control of the emperors, and of government, by marrying their daughters into the imperial family. The Fujiwaras held onto power in Japan for 300 years. During this time the great estates grew bigger and stronger, until the lords ruling them were almost like kings.

The Court of the
Fujiwaras

FACT FILE

A paper-maker at work, spreading wet pulp over a mesh frame. The invention of paper was announced by the director of the Chinese imperial workshops in AD 105. The Chinese began to use paper money under Sung rule.

WHY DID ANCIENT CHINA HAVE SUCH ADVANCED CIVILIZATION?

Chinese cities were a wonder to foreign visitors. Chang'an had more than one million citizens, yet its cleanliness was startling. There were public baths, and hot water was sold in the streets for washing. Toilet facilities in houses were fairly basic, emptying into cesspits, but waste was collected in carts every evening and taken away. The Chinese habit of using toilet paper came as another surprise to visitors.

The Chinese were fascinated by machines. They invented the wheelbarrow for carrying loads, and even fitted barrows with sails to make pushing easier. They used waterwheels to mill rice and drive hammers to beat metal into shape. They knew about the magnetic compass, and their ships had stern rudders. Chinese soldiers had the best crossbows in the world, and smoke and fire weapons.

WHY WERE VIKING LONGSHIPS CRUCIAL TO THEIR RAIDS?

A Viking longship

At a time when sailors dared not venture far from the coasts, the Vikings boldly sailed out, far across the Atlantic in their small open longships. The Viking longships were fast and very strong. They had a long slender hull with a single mast and sail and were very adept at crossing the oceans.

During the 8th century the Viking people began to leave their homes in Scandinavia and explore Europe in search of treasure and places to settle. The Viking invaders are remembered as ruthless raiders and their routes took them throughout Europe and beyond.

FACT FILE

Both Viking men and women dressed in hard-wearing clothing made from linen or woollen cloth. They wore shoes made from leather.

WHY WAS VIKING CULTURE COMPARATIVELY CIVILIZED?

FACT FILE

Decorative brooches such as this were used by both Viking men and women to hold their outer garments (cloaks and tunics) in place.

Viking towns such as Kaupang in Norway and Hedeby in Denmark flourished on deals in furs, reindeer antlers and walrus ivory. These materials were exchanged for weapons, jewels and pottery.

Viking home life was based on farming and fishing. Several generations (including uncles and cousins) often shared one single-roomed house made of wood, stone or turf with a roof thatched with straw. A good sword was highly valued and would be passed down from father to son.

A Viking town

MODERN

HISTORY

CONTENTS

· · · · · · · · · · · · · · · · · · · ·

WHY WAS THE TURKISH LEADER OSMAN SUCCESSFUL?

In about 1300, a Turkish leader called Osman ruled a small kingdom in Anatolia (modern Turkey). His family name in Arabic was 'Othman', and is better known to us today as Ottoman.

Osman and his descendants were to build up one of the most important and long-lasting empires in world history. The Ottoman Turks started to take over parts of the weak Byzantine Empire. The new empire was a strong Muslim answer to the power of Christian Europe in the west.

In 1346 a Byzantine leader hired some Ottomon troops to fight for him, but this turned out to be a big mistake. It allowed the Ottomans to cross into Europe, therefore increasing their empire.

FACT FILE

An intricately carved doorway marks the entrance to an Ottoman mosque.

WHY WAS TIMUR LANG NOTORIOUS?

FACT FILE

When Timur seized the city of Isfahan in 1387, he ordered his men to execute all 7,000 citizens and pile their heads in huge mounds outside the city walls.

Timur Lang (or Timur the Lame), who claimed to be a descendant of Genghis Khan was a ruthless leader. When the Ottomans tried to expand their empire eastwards there was a nasty shock in store for them. Timur had already conquered Persia and ravaged much of central Asia, including Russia and India, before the Ottomans attacked.

Timur fell on the Turks like a hurricane, ransacking their chief city in Anatolia, wiping out their army and capturing their leader. Then he began to loot their empire and break it up. That might have been the end of the Ottoman story, but in 1405 Timur died and the last of the Mongol kingdoms fell apart.

St Peter's Church in Rome

WHY DID THE RENAISSANCE TAKE PLACE?

The Renaissance began in Italy. Rome, the capital city, had been one of the main centres of the classical world. It was full of magnificent old buildings and other objects that inspired the 'rebirth' of culture.

Money was an important reason why the Renaissance started in Italy. The Italian city-states were home to many wealthy families, who were eager to pay for new paintings, sculpture and architecture. Many of the great artists who were available to do the work lived in Italy. They made this one of the most stunningly creative periods in history.

FACT FILE

A column designed by Andrea Palladio, one of the great Renaissance architects. His buildings were designed using classical ideas.

Head of Leda by Leonardo da Vinci

WHY WERE SO MANY ARTISTS LIBERATED IN THE RENAISSANCE ERA?

For the first time since the classical period, artists felt free to show the beauty of the human body. They were helped by two things – the old Greek ideas of proportion and perspective, and the new research on how the body worked. A nude sculpture such as Michelangelo's *David* shows a deep knowledge of the action of muscles, sinews and bones.

A painting of Lorenzo de Medici

Almost all medieval art had depicted religious subjects. Renaissance artists began to paint other things, such as landscapes and scenes of gods and goddesses from mythology. They also painted portraits – of their patrons and of themselves – which expressed human emotions more openly than ever before.

WHY WERE DA VINCI'S IDEAS AHEAD OF HIS TIME?

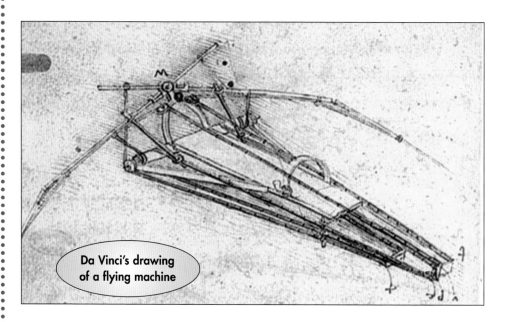

Da Vinci's drawing of a flying machine

During the Renaissance period scientists and inventors were making important discoveries. They were asking questions which would change our view of the Earth – and the Heavens – forever.

Of course not all the inventions actually worked. The great artist and engineer Leonardo da Vinci was determined to find a way of making people fly like birds.

Throughout his life Leonardo da Vinci drew many designs for flying machines. Among these was a kind of parachute and a helicopter with spinning blades. His grandest idea was for an aircraft with flapping wings, which he dreamed up in about 1503. He organized a test flight but according to legend the machine crashed. The first successful aircraft did not actually fly for another 400 years so he was certainly well ahead of his time.

FACT FILE

Galileo Galilei was both an astronomer and a physicist. His observations about the heavens helped to confirm the ideas of Copernicus.

WHY IS COPERNICUS REMEMBERED?

Nicolaus Copernicus was a Polish astronomer. Pictured below is his view of the Universe. He proposed that it was the Sun – not the Earth – which was at the centre of the Universe. The Earth and the other planets simply revolved around it.

His idea was proved correct in the 1620s when the Italian Galileo Galilei used an early telescope to observe the planet Jupiter. He could clearly see that there were other moons in orbit round Jupiter. Here were bodies which were not moving round the Earth. This meant one thing: that the Earth was not the centre of the Universe.

Luther at Wittenberg Castle

WHY DID THE REFORMATION TAKE PLACE?

Martin Luther was a Catholic monk from Germany. In 1510 he visited Rome, the home of the Catholic church, and was deeply shocked. He saw the Pope and his household living in great luxury, and realised the church was bloated with wealth and power. Luther nailed his list of 95 arguments against the church's sale of indulgences to the door of Wittenberg Castle in 1517. His ideas quickly spread across northern Europe. He begged the nobles of Germany to help him reform the old religion. This alarmed the Pope, who sent an order declaring that Luther was a heretic.

FACT FILE

During the Reformation the Bible became available for all to read, thanks to the new printing technology. Also for the first time it was translated from Latin into local languages.

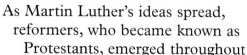

WHY DID KING HENRY VIII DEFY THE POPE?

Henry VIII

As Martin Luther's ideas spread, reformers, who became known as Protestants, emerged throughout Europe. A theological debate followed that eventually erupted into religious warfare that was to last for well over a century.

In England, Henry VIII initially defended the Catholic church. However, the lengths to which Henry VIII went to get a male heir shocked Europe. In 1509, he married Catherine of Aragon, but when all her sons died in infancy, Henry wanted the marriage declared invalid. The Pope refused this request. As a consequence Henry cut all ties between England and the Catholic Church in Rome and declared himself Supreme Head of the Church of England.

FACT FILE

Excommunicated by the Pope, Henry gave himself unrestricted power and set about consolidating the spiritual independence of England from Rome. In 1536, Henry VIII ordered that monasteries such as Tintern Abbey be 'dissolved', or closed down and ransacked.

WHY DID THE SPANISH ARMADA SET OUT TO ATTACK?

Philip of Spain had once hoped to return to England to Catholicism by marrying Queen Elizabeth. She refused him, so he decided to change England's religion by force. In 1588, Philip assembled a fleet of 130 ships and sent them to pick up solders from the Netherlands and invade England. The great Spanish 'Armada' sailed across the English Channel, but never reached its goal. The remnants of the Armada struggled into Spanish ports during autumn 1588.

The defeat of the Armada did not end the war with Spain – it dragged on for another sixteen years.

FACT FILE

Mary Queen of Scots was not a good ruler. In 1568 she was forced to flee Scotland and find refuge in England, throwing herself on the mercy of Elizabeth I.

WHY WAS THE REIGN OF ELIZABETH I SUCCESSFUL?

Despite a traumatic early life – her mother was executed when she was only three and her half-sister Mary had her imprisoned during her brief reign – Elizabeth displayed strength of purpose and prudence as Queen. Strong-willed like her father Henry VIII, but unlike him was fair and grateful to devoted servants, picking advisers who proved able and loyal. In 1559 she pushed through laws which confirmed England as a Protestant nation, with priests ordered to use the new English Prayer Book. Elizabeth ended her reign as one of the best-loved and most successful of all English rulers. Her country was stronger and more peaceful than it had ever been.

FACT FILE

Elizabeth's signature on the death warrant of Mary Stuart. Elizabeth hesitated for days before signing it. She knew that Mary's death would give her Catholic enemies an excuse to attack her.

185

WHY DID THE THIRTY YEARS' WAR TAKE PLACE?

The struggle between Catholics and Protestants in Europe lasted for more than a century. It was made up of a series of great 'wars of religion', which involved countries as far apart as the Netherlands, Spain, Sweden, France and England. The last and biggest of these religious wars began where the Reformation itself had begun – in the bickering states of Germany. This messy conflict became known as the Thirty Years' War.

The war started in a dramatic way. Protestants in Bohemia were angry with their new king, Ferdinand. He wanted to restore Bohemia to the Catholic faith so he closed Protestant schools and ordered Protestant churches in Prague be pulled down. The Protestants banded together and threw some Catholic officials from an upstairs window in Prague Castle. This incident sparked off a civil war in Bohemia.

Defenestration of Prague

FACT FILE

This matchlock musket gun is a typical weapon used by infantry soldiers during the Thirty Years' War.

WHY WAS THE PALACE OF VERSAILLES BUILT?

FACT FILE

The master Dutch painter Rembrandt van Rijn was at work during the period of the Thirty Years' War. He produced a great number of works of art, including around 600 paintings and about 100 self-portraits.

In the 17th century, Louis XIV of France was famous for his power and wealth. He was the most important monarch in Europe. The palace that was built for him at Versailles, outside Paris, became the model for palaces throughout the continent.

It took forty-seven years to build and was renowned for its extreme grandeur. Great crystal chandeliers hung from the ceilings, their candlelight reflected in gilded mirrors. Fine tapestries and paintings decorated the walls. There is an emblem of the Sun on the main gate of the palace. It portrays Louis as the 'Sun King'.

187

WHY DID A FARMING REVOLUTION TAKE PLACE?

In 1700 more than 90 percent of Europe's population lived in the countryside. Most were peasants working on the land. They grew their own food, using tools and farming methods which had changed very little since medieval times. By 1800 the number of people in Europe soared from 120 million to over 180 million. Farmers needed to find ways to grow much bigger quantities of crops so that there was enough food to feed many more people.

FACT FILE

As a result of improved breeding techniques, farmers were able to produce sheep which gave better wool. They also had short legs and barrel-like bodies for more meat.

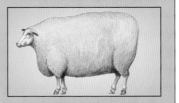

turnips

barley

clover

WHY DID THE PRACTICE OF CROP ROTATION PROVE SUCCESSFUL?

The medieval system of growing crops was wasteful. By about 1650, Dutch farmers had developed a more efficient way of 'rotating' their crops. Instead of leaving a field fallow, they made it fertile more quickly by spreading manure or growing clover and grasses to improve the soil.

In the 1730s, farmers such as Charles Townshend of England, began using a four-part system of planting crops in rotation. In this system wheat was grown in the first year and turnips in the second. Sheep or cattle ate the turnips, providing valuable manure. Barley was sown in the third year, then grass or clover. This method was widely adopted and became known as the 'four-course crop rotation system'.

Four-course crop rotation

wheat

FACT FILE

Since farming began, farmers had scattered seed by hand. Jethro Tull's seed drill put the seed directly into the soil in neat rows.

WHY DID MACHINES AND FACTORIES TAKE OVER PRODUCTION?

Ironworks at Coalbrookdale

During the 1700s the whole world was speeding up, populations were growing, and these extra people needed more food, more homes and more jobs.

At the same time, industry was expanding at an amazing rate, thanks to the development of new machines, new methods of making things and new sources of power. The result was a dramatic change in the way people lived and worked. Machines in factories created millions of new jobs, so many people began to leave the countryside to work in towns. We call this change the Industrial Revolution.

FACT FILE

Whitney's cotton gin machine was a simple way of cleaning raw cotton. It brushed out the seeds from the cotton fibres.

WHY WERE DAVY LAMPS USED?

During the time of the Industrial Revolution, coal became increasingly important as the fuel for ovens and forges. Coal mines were dug deeper as demand grew, leading to greater dangers of floods, collapse and gas explosions. Inventions such as Newcomen's steam pump (to remove water) and Davy's safety lamp eased these problems.

Davy's safety lamp warned miners of gas leaks underground. Inventions such as this only encouraged coal miners to go into farther and more dangerous depths.

Abraham Darby's discovery that coal could be turned into coke led to the production of coke-smelted iron. The improved iron could be used to make everything from ploughs and bridges to steam engines and drilling machines.

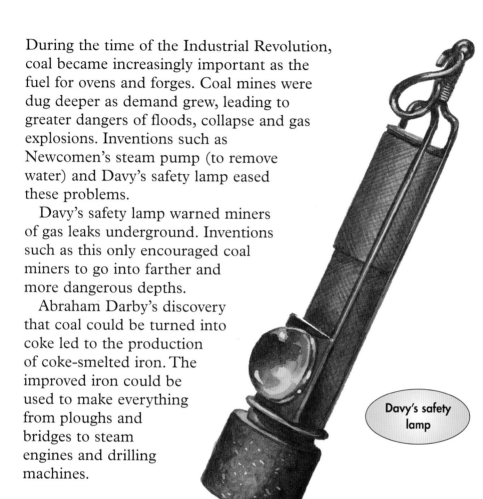

Davy's safety lamp

FACT FILE

Benjamin Franklin was an American statesman as well as a scientist. Franklin proved that lightning and electricity are the same thing by flying a kite in a storm. He was struck by lightning and was lucky to survive.

WHY DID THE AMERICAN REVOLUTION TAKE PLACE?

FACT FILE

The American flag. The 13 red and white stripes, and the 13 stars, stood for the 13 original colonies that signed the Declaration of Independence. The modern American flag has 50 stars, one for each state.

The Seven Years' War saw the end of French power in North America. By 1763 more than two million British colonists were living there. These people now wanted to be able to govern themselves.

Britain, however, had different ideas about her colonies, because they were an important market for trade. A large British army and naval fleet was still stationed to protect North America. The British government was concerned about who was going to pay for these forces. The answer was the colonists themselves – through new and increased taxes.

American victory at Saratoga in 1777.

WHY DID THE BOSTON TEA PARTY TAKE PLACE?

The British government imposed several new taxes, on things as different as official paper and molasses. The Americans had never been taxed before, and protested loudly. Some of the taxes were removed, but import duties on luxury goods such as tea were increased. The Americans had no-one to put their case democratically to the parliament in London, so they decided to take direct action for themselves.

In 1773, a band of colonists seized three British ships in Boston harbour, Massachusetts and dumped their cargo of tea overboard. This became known as the 'Boston Tea Party'. It enraged the British government, who sent troops to put Massachusetts under military rule.

FACT FILE

In 1775 George Washington was elected as commander-in-chief of the colonists' army. To many Americans at that time, he became a leading symbol of their fight for independence.

WHY DID NAPOLEON TAKE FRANCE TO WAR?

After years of political dispute and unrest, the French people welcomed Napoleon as their new leader in 1799. Not only was Napoleon a brilliant general, he also proved himself to be a skilful administrator.

Although Europe was at peace briefly in 1802, Napoleon, after abandoning attempts to increase French influence in North America, turned his attention to expanding his empire in Europe. To raise money, he sold a huge area of land in North America, called Louisiana, to the Americans. In 1803, France and Britain went to war again.

FACT FILE

Napoleon is considered to be a great military genius, and one of the greatest commanders in history. Yet he was also described as an 'enemy and disturber of the peace of the world'.

Napoleon wanted to land an army in Britain, so he needed to control the seas. But in 1805, a British fleet under Lord Nelson defeated the combined French and Spanish fleets at the battle of Trafalgar. This defeat ended Napoleon's hopes of invading Britain.

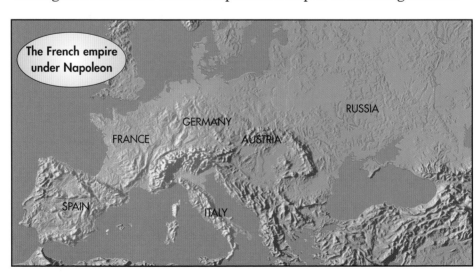

The French empire under Napoleon

RUSSIA

GERMANY

FRANCE

AUSTRIA

SPAIN

ITALY

The battle of Waterloo

WHY WAS THE BATTLE OF WATERLOO A SIGNIFICANT LOSS TO THE FRENCH?

By 1812, Napoleon had created a French empire that covered almost the whole of Europe. However, after a disastrous campaign in Russia Napoleon's empire began to crumble. In April 1814, Napoleon was forced to abdicate. He went into exile in Elba, an island off the coast of Italy, only to return with fresh troops the following year to make another bid for power. The combined armies of Britain, Austria, Prussia and Russia defeated Napoleon's army at the battle of Waterloo in 1815. It was to be Napoleon's last battle. The French had more soldiers and better artillery but they were still soundly beaten. He was sent into exile on the island of St Helena, where he died in 1821.

FACT FILE

Napoleon's distinctive hat. Napoleon was a great military strategist, who seemed instinctively to know the best time to attack during a battle.

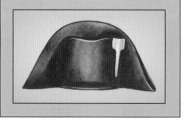

WHY DID GARIBALDI UNIFY ITALY?

The Treaty of Paris that brought the Crimean War to an end did little to bring stability to Europe. The leader of Sardinia-Piedmont, Count Cavour, used the meetings at Paris to demand unification for Italy. At that time, Italy was made up of many separate states, most controlled by Austria. The movement for independence, known as the Risorgimento, started in the 1820s and 1830s. In 1858, Sardinia-Piedmont allied itself with France and drove out the Austrians from much of northern Italy. The successful revolt by Guiseppe Garibaldi and his 'red shirts' led eventually to the unification of all of Italy. Italy was declared a kingdom under King Victor-Emmanuel II in 1861. Rome was captured and made the capital of a unified Italy in 1871.

FACT FILE

Paris in 1848. People took to the streets to demand a new republic as well as votes for all males. Government soldiers shot and killed some of the rioters.

WHY IS FLORENCE NIGHTINGALE REMEMBERED?

Florence Nightingale was an English nurse who single-handedly revolutionized nursing practices, sanitation in hospitals and public health in the 19th century.

When war broke out in the Crimea, Nightingale volunteered for duty, leaving with 38 nurses in her charge. She organized the barracks hospital after the Battle of Inkerman, and by introducing discipline and hygiene to hospitals she managed to reduce the death toll. When she returned to England in 1856, she was rewarded with a fund of £50,000 for training nurses.

FACT FILE

Florence Nightingale was known as the 'Lady with the Lamp' because of the light she carried at night. She would walk through the hospital corridors, checking on her patients.

WHY DID THE FAMINE IN IRELAND BEGIN?

At the beginning of the 1800s, the population of Ireland stood at about five million. In the first 40 years of the century the population increased to about eight million. Many people lived in extreme poverty. In 1845 a fungus affected the vital potato crop in southern England, which soon spread to Ireland. With the failure of the potato crop, people began to die in their thousands either from hunger or disease.

The famine came to an end after 1849 when the potato crop only partially failed. By then the population of Ireland had been reduced to just over six million by famine and emigration.

FACT FILE

When Ireland's potato crop failed, people dug up their crops only to find them rotting in the ground. Others picked what looked like sound potatoes, but they simply went rotten later on.

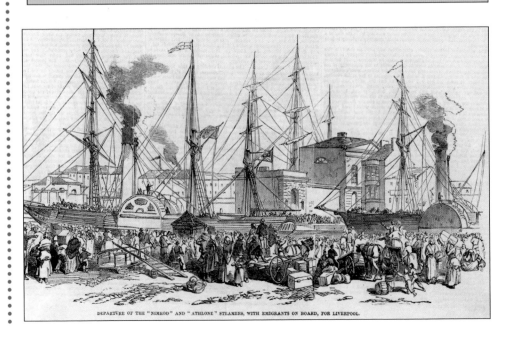

DEPARTURE OF THE "NIMROD" AND "ATHLONE" STEAMERS, WITH EMIGRANTS ON BOARD, FOR LIVERPOOL.

WHY DID GLADSTONE NOT HELP THE IRISH?

The British prime minister, Sir Robert Peel, organized relief for the poorest people of Ireland during the famine. This enabled them to be able to buy cheap corn imported from the United States. It helped to prevent many people from starving to death. But it was a different story when Peel resigned.

William Gladstone was the dominant figure in Britain's Liberal Party from 1868 to 1894. He was actually prime minister four times during the reign of Queen Victoria. His belief was that Ireland should run their own affairs, and was a strong supporter of Home Rule.

Supporters of Home Rule wanted a separate parliament to deal with Irish affairs in Dublin.

FACT FILE

Irish politician Charles Parnell addresses an audience in support of Home Rule. He became leader of the Home Rule Party in the British parliament, and fought tirelessly for his beliefs. Parnell was even imprisoned by the British for a time.

WHY DID THE SUFFRAGETTE MOVEMENT TAKE PLACE?

During war time women were brought in to fill the jobs of those men that had gone to fight in the war. The poster (shown here on the right) emphasized the important role women had to play. In 1893, New Zealand became the first country in the world to allow women to vote in national elections. Australia followed suit in 1903, and Finland in 1906. In other parts of the world, however, women were engaged in a bitter and often violent battle for the right to vote.

In Britain, Emmeline Pankhurst founded the Women's Social and Political Union in 1903. The WSPU believed in actions rather than words, and many of its members, known as suffragettes, were arrested and imprisoned. One suffragette called Emily Davison was killed when she threw herself beneath the king's horse at a race.

FACT FILE

In Britain, the suffragette campaigners often went on hunger strike when imprisoned for their actions. The authorities did not want the suffragettes to die – and arouse public sympathy – so they fed the women by force.

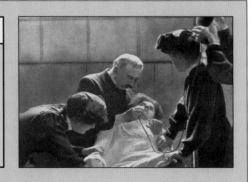

Emmeline Pankhurst being arrested

WHY DID WWI AID THE PLIGHT OF EQUAL RIGHTS FOR WOMEN?

FACT FILE

The suffragettes engaged in many different forms of protest, from interrupting public meetings by shouting slogans to chaining themselves to railings outside the residence of the British prime minister.

World War I was a turning-point in many countries for the women's movement. During the war, women had filled the places of the men who had gone off to fight, working in industries such as munitions factories, on farms as labourers, and in the mines. After the end of the war, equal voting rights were introduced in Canada (1918), Austria, Czechoslovakia, Germany and Poland (1919), and in 1920 in Hungary and the USA. The right to vote was extended to all women over the age of 21 in 1928. Emmeline Pankhurst, founder of the WSPU, died a month after British women gained equal voting rights.

WHY DID WAR BREAK OUT IN 1914?

FACT FILE

A World War I gas mask. After the Germans used poisonous gas for the first time in April 1915, masks became an essential part of every soldier's kit.

As the 19th century drew to a close, rivalry increased between the different nations of Europe.

In June 1914, the heir to the Austro-Hungarian throne, Archduke Franz Ferdinand, and his wife Sophie made a tour of Bosnia. As they drove through the streets of Sarajevo, a Serbian assassin shot them both dead. In retaliation, Austria-Hungary, backed by Germany, declared war on Serbia. Soon all the major European powers were drawn into the conflict. Russia, backed by France, supported Serbia. Then Germany invaded neutral Belgium and attacked France, drawing Britain into the conflict.

WHY DID THE USA ENTER THE WAR IN 1915?

From the start of the Great War, the name by which World War I was first known, British warships blockaded German ports. In this way Britain's navy prevented supplies from reaching Germany, causing severe shortages of food and other goods. The Germans retaliated with their submarines, called U-boats. After 1915, U-boats attacked both warships and merchant shipping carrying supplies to Britain. In May 1915, a German torpedo hit a British passenger ship called the *Lusitania*. The ship was carrying nearly 2,000 passengers, including many Americans. The sinking of the Lusitania was one of the factors that eventually drew the United States into the war.

TELL ME WHY : MODERN HISTORY

WHY DID THE BATTLE OF BRITAIN TAKE PLACE?

The evacuation from Dunkerque

In March 1939, the German leader Adolf Hitler threatened to invade Poland. Both Great Britain and France gave guarantees to help Poland if it was attacked. So when Hitler invaded Poland on September 1, 1939 Britain and France were forced to declare war on Germany. The majority of the British army was saved in 1940 by a desperate evacuation from the French port of Dunkerque.

The Battle of Britain began in July 1940 between the German airforce, the Luftwaffe, and Britain's Royal Air Force (RAF). Nightly air raids that took place in the autumn and winter of 1940–1941 are known as the Blitz. However, by May 1941 the RAF had gained the upper hand, and Hitler gave up the attempt to bomb Britain into submission – although air raids continued throughout the war.

FACT FILE

The Battle of Britain was the world's first major air battle. The British fighter planes were able to shoot down many of the long-range German bomber aircraft, shown here.

WHY WERE THE D-DAY LANDINGS A TURNING POINT IN THE WAR?

TELL ME WHY : MODERN HISTORY

FACT FILE

Charles de Gaulle was leader of the French troops, known as the Free French, who had escaped occupied France. After the war he became one of France's most powerful presidents ever.

In June 1944, Allied leaders decided that it was time to attack Germany itself. Under the overall command of US General Eisenhower, Allied troops landed in Normandy and advanced across France. Meanwhile, Soviet troops moved across eastern Europe.

On the morning of 6 June, 1944, thousands of Allied troops went ashore along the coast of Normandy in northern France in what became known as the D-Day landings.

D-Day landings

The Damascus Gate

WHY WAS ISRAEL CREATED?

At the end of World War II, the demands for a Jewish state in Palestine grew. In 1947, the United Nations took over responsibility for Palestine, dividing it into an Arab state and a Jewish state. The Jews agreed to this plan, but the Arabs did not. The state of Israel came into being on May 14, 1948. It was immediately attacked by Arab armies from Egypt, Syria, Lebanon, Iraq and Transjordan (Jordan) – known collectively as the Arab League. By 1949, Israel had defeated the Arab League and added land to its own territory.

FACT FILE

Civil war broke out between Christians and Muslims in the Lebanon in 1975. Fighting caused extensive damage in Beirut.

WHY WAS THE COLD WAR STARTED?

After World War II, the United States and the USSR (Union of Soviet Socialist Republics) emerged as the two main powers in the world – known as 'superpowers'. Although they had fought together to defeat Nazi Germany, differences between the two superpowers soon led to the start of the 'Cold War'.

The Cold War was a political war between the USSR and its communist allies, and the USA and other non-communist countries. It did not involve fighting, although there was a threat of military action on several occasions.

The Berlin airlift